Well-Being, Transcendence, Longevity And Happiness Through Breathing:

The Secret of Breathing

Dr. H. Prashad

Books For All

Delhi-110052

© Har Prashad

First Published 2018

ISBN 13: 978-81-7386-318-9
ISBN 10: 81-7386-318-0

Published By
BOOKS FOR ALL
(an imprint of Low Price Publications)
A-6, Second Floor, Nimri Commercial Centre,
Ashok Vihar Phase-4, Delhi - 110 052
Tel.: +91 11 2730 2453
website: www.Lppindia.com
e-mail: info@Lppindia.com

Printed At
D K Fine Art Press P Ltd.
Phone: 27302929

PRINTED IN INDIA

Dedicated To

The Almighty, Cosmic Power, Supernal and Silence Formless Oneness, whose Blessings, Radiance, Continued Inspiration, Booming Energy and Silent Guidance that has graced me to follow the path of Peace and Enlightenment for realizing the Ultimate Truth and Self – Realization; and to be always being in Him and to be beyond Time & Space for ultimate mergence in the "Being", the Absolute.

March 2016   Dr. Har Prashad

Preface

Human life revolves around breathing. Life is extinguished as breath leaves the body. Secret of breath is life. One can live without food and water for couple of days but not without breathe even for a nano second. Breath is replica of God; breath is master. Proper breathing gives heath, longevity and happiness to a human being. It is the cause of well-being and transcendence of time & space. The book on "Well-Being, Transcendence, Longevity and Happiness through Breathing—The Secret of Breathing" analyses various aspects of breathing, its benefits besides its close co-ordination with medical science for welfare of human body.

The book also brings out and analyzes the subtle aspects of breathing that are closely linked with mind, body and spirit. The book is brought with scientific background by self experience with the art of breathing along with study of multifaceted aspects of existing knowledge on breathing analyzing its various unique aspects to serve the humanity.

The secret of breathing in the book has brought out the various inner physiological transformation during the stage of mergence/ Samadhi when consciousness has transcended time and space. Also, appropriate ways and means for breathing have been scientifically analyzed for physical well-being, longevity and happiness.

In brief, various aspects of dormant human science on breathing have been analyzed and are classified in various chapters of this book, which deeply concern to human being and has close relation with knowledge, wisdom and understanding of the art of breathing for transcendence of time & space. These are also the tools and prerequisites, which may be helpful in extension of life span along with health and happiness.

The art of breathing is the universal knowledge of subjective science, which is applicable to each one of us. This knowledge leads to overall physical and mental development without any negative aspects and enhance the well-being. Also, this prepares oneself for transcendence to travel beyond time and space

No other approach and science may be as universal as this. However, this is subjective science; one alone has to adopt and develop it personally very gradually to manifest this art. No body else can help; only technique, ways and means are brought forward that may assist.

Furthermore, various aspects of the science of art of breathing assists to take step into "Being" by a being, which have been analyzed with proper modulation and evolved contemplation with philosophical churning to make it understandable for easy perception, adaptation and implementation. This book is unique in many ways and directions since it contains the essence of various complex subjects that revolves around the art of breathing for health, happiness, longevity and well-being besides transcendence of "time & space" with discontinuities, which is a sole mean to manifest consciousness.

The book contains multifaceted chapters by retrieval of the concept of dormant human science in the light of present day understanding so that it can be used for the enhancement of health and happiness with in depth understanding of self and to be self-realized. The book includes various chapters covering mysterious topics in details including: consciousness & conscious breathing; breath control - a ladder for personality transformation; breathe is life; secret of breath; breathing- medical view point; abdominal breathing; mindfulness of breathing; chi energy and Prana.

The art of breathing and various techniques of breathing have been included for in-depth understanding of discontinuity in breathing; breath—a tool to control mind; breath suspension- an art to achieve silence; tranquil breath to control stresses; linkage between breath and happiness; pranas and evolution—mystery of breath; well-being, health, happiness, transcendence and life extension through breathing; breath — the invisible divine force & energy; enlightenment through cessation of breath for realization and welfare of a human being.

The book also covers the visualization of mystery of life and death through breath; experiencing death within life through breathing; to be in present through breathing; dhyana/meditation by witnessing the breath; breath and quantum jump; breathe— mystery of relaxation; transcendence of time & space by breath; evolution through Kriya yoga—the regulated breathing process; awakening of Kundalini power through breath and pranas; means to overcome boredom and egoism through art of breathing besides sandhya & mystery of void and breath etc.

As I understand, no book covering many diversifying topics concerning human life for welfare of mankind along with the art, philosophy and various techniques for breathing, manifestation of consciousness and wisdom has appeared so far. Furthermore, this book gives rare knowledge of human interest for self-evolution, enlightenment, realization, art of happiness, transcendence of time & space and to be with the "Being", which is the source of knowledge, creativity and creation.

Finally, I would like to express my gratitude to the Cosmic Power; Cosmic Consciousness; Almighty; Universal "Being", who has infused me to take up this accomplishment and boomed me with the Source of untiring and inexhaustible energy; Radiance; Creativity; Continued Inspiration and Silence guidance. This has nurtured me all the time to follow and pursue the path to be beyond time & space to manifest consciousness with discontinuities to be with the "Being", and to offer to mankind the unique path for their welfare, health, longevity and transcendence.

Also, I would like to acknowledge silent participation of my wife, Darshan; son and daughter-in-law Poojan & Gauri with delicate new arrival Kavish; daughter and son-in-law Shweta & Rajeev with little Kriya & loving Rohan Nimay to climb the ladder of this accomplishment.

Vancouver   Dr. Har Prashad
March 2016

12533 South Surrey   302 Central View

28th Avenue   Domal Guda

V4a 2n8   Hyderabad-500029

Canada   India

Mobile: 1-604-825-5139 (Canada)

Mobile: 91-9652013280 (India)

Email: har.prashad@gmail.com

About the Author

Dr. Har Prashad is presently advisor and consultant on Tribology. He is retired Senior Deputy General Manager (Tribology) from the Bharat Heavy Electricals Limited (BHEL), Corporate Research and Development Division, Hyderabad (India) in 2004. He was consultant of Centre for Tribology Inc (CETR), USA till August 2011 and advisor to Rtec, USA till 2015. He obtained an M.E. (Hons) degree in Mechanical Engineering in 1970, and subsequently, Ph.D. in Tribology. He worked with the Indian Institute of Petroleum, Dehra Dun, and with the Design Bureau at Bokaro Steel Ltd., Dahnbad, Bihar, before joining BHEL in 1974.

Dr. Prashad has published more than 125 papers in both national and international journals, reviewed more than 200 technical papers and many Ph.D. thesis. For his achievements, author's name has been included in Marquis Who's Who in the world published in 2001 and 2012 from USA. Also, his name was included in International Directory of Distinguished Leadership-2001, published by American Biographical Institute. His bio-data is published in the directory of "Contemporary Who's who 2004" and in 2012 by the same institute. Also, "Scientific Award of Excellence 2011" has been awarded by the same Institute. Furthermore, for his distinguished achievements Tribology Society of India graced him with Life Time Achievement Award 2010 (Industrial Category) in the Seventh International Conference on Industrial Tribology-2010, held at Ranchi (Organized by Sail Authority of India under the Aegis of Tribology Society of India) on 4th December 2010. He was the Vice President of Tribology Society of India, and also Honorary President of Kriya Yoga Centre of Hyderabad till 2014. He is in the panel member to review articles for publication in international technical journals.

He is the author of seven technical books and seventeen books on human sciences. The books are:

* "Tribology in Electrical Environments" Published from United Kingdom by Elsevier Publishers in December 2005.

* "Solving Tribology Problems of Rotating Machines" Published by Wood head Publishers, U.K, in February 2006.

* "Integral Approaches to Tribo-testing in Mechanical Engineering" Published by CRC, USA in August 2009.

* "Behaviour of Rolling-element Bearings under Shaft Voltages" Published by Lambert Academic Publishing, Germany in 2011.

* "Electrical Analogy of Different types of Journal & Thrust Bearings", Published by Lambert Academic Publishing, 2011.

* "A System Approach to Mechanical Engineering Problems", Published by Lambert Academic Publishing, 2011.

* "Anti-friction Bearings and Lubricants under Electrical Currents", Published by Lambert Academic Publishing, 2012.

* "Solutions of Problems & Remedies of Human Life—A Path of Peace And Enlightenment", Published by Books For All (an Imprint of Low Price Publications, Delhi, India), 2010.

* "Japu Ji Sahib and Srimad Bhagavad-Gita – The Spark of Enlightenment", Published by Books For All (an Imprint of Low Price Publications, Delhi, India), 2011.

* "Spikes of Deep Silence by Silence and in Silence", Published by Books For All (an Imprint of Low Price Publications, Delhi, India), 2012.

* E-book on "Know Thyself - A Guide for Spiritual Aspirants" Published By Yellow Bay of U.K., 2011.

* "Dormant Human Science—Science and Philosophy", Published by Lambert Academic Publishing, Germany, January 2012.

* "Mysterious Life Waves—Science and Philosophy", Published by Lambert Academic Publishing, 2012

* "Unison at Core—Mergence in Oneness", Published by Lambert Academic Publishing, 2012.

* "Retrieving the Immersed Subjective Science—Path of Inner Evolution", Published by Lambert Academic Publishing, 2012.

* "Multifaceted Approach of being Conscious and Creative—The Integral Vision", Published by Lambert Academic Publishing, 2012.

* "Life is Continuum with Discontinuities—Glimpses of Self in Self", Published by Lambert Academic Publishing, 2012.

* "Scientific Integration of Queries on Inner Human Life", Published by Books For All (an Imprint of Low Price Publications, Delhi, India), 2013.

* "Life Extension through Manifestation of Consciousness—Transcendence of Time & Space with Discontinuities", Published by Lambert Academic Publishing, 2013.

* "Discontinuities in Continuities to Evolution in Realm of Life—Source Of Subtle Wisdom", Published by Lambert Academic Publishing, 2013.

* "Breath is Master—Health, Happiness and Transcendence through Breathing", Published by Lambert Academic Publishing, 2014.

* "Improved Longevity of Life by Evolution of Consciousness", Published by Shiva Publishing House, India, 2014.

* "Principle Jewels of Life to Enlightenment—Fragrance of the Unknown," Published by Books For All (an Imprint of Low Price Publications, Delhi, India), 2015.

* "Perceive, Realize and Implement to Evolve in Life - Fragrance of Subtle Virtues from the Unknown", Published by Lambert Academic Publishing, June 2016.

Contents

1

Introduction

This book on "Well-being, Transcendence, Longevity and Happiness through Breathing—The Secret of Breathing" revolves around various benefits brought out by breathing in medical sciences, yoga, and spiritual sciences. All these are highly evolved sciences; they are mutually interwoven; however, they are not well coordinated with each other very deeply as to how miraculously these can uplift well-being of human being to enhance health, longevity and happiness; and to manifest the consciousness by transcendence of time & space through the art of proper breathing.

Medical research in breathing science has brought multifaceted benefits to human body through proper breathing; yoga has put forward tangible means of physical cure through proper stretching with controlled breathing. However, consciousness, a very significant component of human existence, which is the core of spiritual science and deeply interwoven with breathing process has not been well analyzed and understood.

Although being conscious in breathing; maintaining full consciousness in breathing process, all subtle energies of infinite universal/cosmic consciousness unite with human consciousness; this enriches health, happiness, well being and increases subtle virtues in human life. Along with this, however, basic health laws of good nourishing food, proper exercise and stress free life play a major role and these have to be followed judicially.

Furthermore, it has been brought out that type of breath plays a very important role in well-being, longevity and manifestation of consciousness. Breath is considered as Master since without breath one cannot survive even for a micro second; however, without food and water one can survive couple of days.

Proper breathing can control stresses; one can be at peace and control his mind since mind and breath are very closely related; mind gets subtle energy through breath. So, breath control and regulation of breathe can easily influence mind; it can control anger; depression; it gives energy to the system. Pranayama is known technique for regulated breath in the art of yoga; its role to enhance the health of human being is well established.

Calm and slow flow of breath reduces fatigue life of the human system and enhances life span. If one is consciously witnessing the flow of breath; one can easily concentrate; it helps to sleep and it is tool to go to deep sleep. Various aspects of breathing pattern, types of breaths have been deeply analyzed.

One can transcendence time & space by witnessing the breath. Increase in discontinuity between breathe in and breathe out enhances the subtle energy in the system. Breath is the source of prana, life force and proper functioning of the human system. It can cure many illnesses of the physical body and keeps the subtle bodies in harmonious state through the subtle energies generated by proper breathing process.

Controlled breath is a ladder for personality transformation; suspension of breath is a mode to step in the zone of silence and means to be beyond time & space. Proper regulation of breath acts as a tool to arise the dormant Kundalini power in the human system. It is the means to bestow enlightenment. All these aspects, as perceived, have been brought out.

Breath is Master; it guides to take step in to "Being"; one cannot live without breath. Happiness is instantaneous breathless state; this state cannot be prolonged to exist; without breath and without "Being" there is no existence; so happiness is transient and it can be made permanent till one is with the "Being". Various such aspects have been deeply dealt in details in different chapters.

Medical research has recognized the tangible benefits of abdominal breathing; mindfulness of breathing; and breathing through the whole system. Consciousness as a new dimension is needed to be included in future research to study the effect of conscious breathing on overall human system; its effect on mind and various incurable and unknown diseases, which are increasing day by day.

It is perceived that consciousness/awareness may act as vigilance on breathing process so as to check the unknown subtle virus ingredients being inhaled by mechanical breathing process. This might have an observer effect as discovered in quantum physics.

After self experiencing of various benefits of conscious breathing on subtle qualities, it is expected that it might have close relations with physical ailment and overall well-being apart from achieving mental peace and happiness. Conscious breathing, if scientifically diagnosed, may open a new era in medical treatment. However, breath is life and scientific views on various aspects of breathing on well-being are very encouraging.

Adding new dimension of conscious breathing may play an immense holistic role for well-being of human being. However, subtle changes by controlled breathing have been duly experienced and recognized by spiritual science.

Present need is to pursue cohesive movement of spiritual and medical sciences so that breathing techniques and its tangible benefits shall become universal approach to serve the human-race by a defined spiritual-medical science.

In short, benefits of proper and controlled breathing have been projected in different chapters of this book in multifaceted manners as conceived and experienced for health , happiness, longevity, well-being and transcendence of time & space for manifestation of consciousness to enhance subtle qualities; and to be with the "Being".

2

Breathing–Medical View Point

The primary role of breathing is gas exchange: our cells need oxygen and their waste product, carbon dioxide, needs to be expelled. Breathing is an automatic body function, controlled by the respiratory centre of the brain. However, we can also deliberately change our rate of breathing.

Different healing systems, from different cultures, have long realized the healing benefits of the breath, including yoga, Tai Chi and some forms of meditation. Many holistic practitioners believe that the breath is the link between the physical body and the ethereal mind, and spiritual insight is possible through conscious breathing.

Regardless of the philosophy, scientific studies have shown that correct breathing can help to manage stress and stress-related conditions by soothing the autonomic nervous system. Stress can be managed and reduced with proper breathing. Shallow breathing is a typical stress response. Hyperventilation can prolong anxiety and stress.

Abdominal breathing techniques soothe the nervous system and encourage health benefits, such as reduced blood pressure.

The use of controlled breathing as a means of promoting relaxation can help to manage a range of disorders, including:

Anxiety

Asthma

Chronic fatigue syndrome

Chronic pain

High blood pressure

Insomnia

Panic attacks

Some skin conditions, such as eczema

And Stress.

To stay inflated, the lungs rely on a vacuum inside the chest. The diaphragm is a sheet of muscle slung underneath the lungs. When we breathe, the diaphragm contracts and relaxes. This change in pressure means that air is 'sucked' into the lungs on inhalation and 'pushed' out of the lungs on exhalation.

The intercostals' muscles between the ribs help to change the internal pressure by lifting and relaxing the rib cage in rhythm with the diaphragm. Flexing the diaphragm requires the use of the lower abdominal. If one's abdomen gently moves in and out while he breathes, then he is breathing correctly.

Furthermore, the brain sets the breathing rate according to carbon dioxide levels, rather than oxygen levels. When a person is under stress, his breathing pattern changes. Typically, an anxious person takes small and shallow breaths using his shoulders rather than his diaphragm to move air in and out of his lungs.

This style of breathing empties too much carbon dioxide out of the blood and changes the body's balance of gases. Shallow over-breathing - or hyper-ventilation - can prolong feelings of anxiety by exacerbating physical symptoms of stress, including:

Chest tightness;

Constant fatigue;

Faintness and light-headedness;

Feelings of panic;

Headaches;

Heart palpitations;

Insomnia;

Muscular aches, twitches or stiffness;

Tingling numb cold hands and face.

Moreover, when a person is relaxed, his breathing is nasal, slow, even and gentle. Deliberately mimicking a relaxed breathing pattern seems to calm the autonomic nervous system, which governs involuntary bodily functions. Physiological changes through relax breathing can include:

Lowered blood pressure and heart rate;

Reduced amounts of stress hormones;

Reduced lactic acid build-up in muscle tissue;

Balanced levels of oxygen and carbon dioxide in the blood;

Improved immune system functioning;

Increased physical energy;

Manifesting a feeling of calmness, and well-being.

There are different breathing techniques to bring about relaxation. In essence, the general aim is to shift from upper chest breathing to abdominal breathing. Take notice of how your upper chest and abdomen are moving while you breathe.

Concentrate on your breath and try to breathe in and out gently through the nose. Your upper chest and stomach should be still, allowing the diaphragm to work more efficiently with your abdomen and less with your chest.

With each breath, allow any tension in your body to slip away. Once you are breathing slowly with your abdomen, sit quietly and enjoy the sensation of physical relaxation.

One must remember:

Shallow, upper chest breathing is part of the typical stress response.

The stress response can be switched off by consciously breathing with the diaphragm.

Abdominal breathing plugs into the autonomic nervous system and encourages it to relax, bringing a range of health benefits.

3

Breath of Life

The first step in healthy breathing is to become conscious of how we actually breathe. From the perspective of the world's great spiritual traditions, our breath not only brings needed oxygen and other gases to the physical body, but it can also bring, when we are conscious of it, the finer energies (prana, chi, and so on) needed to help nourish our higher bodies–the subtle body, causal body, and so on.

Whatever we may believe about our soul and spirit, our breath, and how we breathe, is intimately connected with all aspects of our being.

In today's noisy, high-stress world, many of us sit, stand, sleep, speak, act, and move in ways that undermine our breathing and our physical, emotional, and spiritual health. When we look at ourselves in action, when we actually sense and observe ourselves honestly for a moment, we see that we carry enormous amounts of unnecessary tension throughout our bodies.

We may sense it in our hands, face, eyes, jaw, tongue, throat, belly, back, chest, and so on (even tension in our feet can undermine our breathing). These tensions can and often do impede the natural, harmonious movement of the diaphragm and its coordination with the secondary breathing muscles. They also impede the harmonious flow of the breath of life through our body/mind.

We can do all the breathing exercises in the world, but if we don't begin to see and free ourselves from the unnecessary tensions that we carry day in and day out—if we are unable to find a state of dynamic relaxation in the midst of daily living—these exercises won't do much good.

In fact, without such relaxation and without real self-knowledge and self-awareness, breathing exercises can often exacerbate the tensions already present and create dangerous biochemical and physiological imbalances in our body/mind.

In beginning to study these unnecessary tensions in ourselves, which are generated in large part by our mostly unconscious attitudes toward ourselves and others, one of the most useful situations with which to begin is when we find ourselves in a hurry, which, for many of us, is almost all the time.

Next time you catch yourself rushing through your life on the way some place other than where you are right now (and this can be a mental or emotional "rushing" as well as a physical one), sense your entire body and pay particular attention to your breathing. What does your breath feel like? Does it feel open and spacious? Most likely it feels small and cramped.

Ask yourself if this is really how you want to live your life, always tensing toward something to be done or enjoyed (or something you believe will be better) in the future. Yes, the future is important and we all have plenty to do on its behalf, but what's the point of all this "doing" if we don't actually feel and appreciate the pure miracle of our aliveness, our being, right here and now?

What's the point of all of this activity if we are not open enough to receive and appreciate the life force flowing through us and others and the rich scale of impressions and perceptions that come with it?

It is only through a constant deep felt appreciation of the value and miracle of being itself that our lives will take on real meaning, that our relationships with others will become imbued with intelligence and compassion, and that we will find effective solutions to the ever-growing problems we face.

If we are constantly filled with unnecessary tension based on judgments about the past and expectations about the future, our breath will remain cramped and disharmonious, we will never discover what it means to be truly human, and our lives on this planet will only get worse no matter what brilliant strategies we devise or how much force and aggression we use to put them into action.

To see and release the unnecessary tensions that fill our lives, and to allow the breath of life to manifest fully through us and others, begins with sensing and observing ourselves at this very moment, paying special attention to the tensions that propel us through time, as well as the inner attitudes that fuel them.

It begins with being present to "what is," without any self-deception. This is the beginning of real transformation, both for our selves personally and for the world. And it all begins with awareness of the breath.

One of the safest and most powerful breathing practices or exercises you can undertake is to consciously follow your breathing in the many changing circumstances of your life. As you inhale, simply be aware that you are inhaling. As you exhale, simply be aware that you are exhaling. Try this exercise for 10 minutes or so at a time at least three times a day.

It will help free you from your automatic thoughts and emotional reactions and thus enable you to live with more receptivity and clarity in the present moment. You may find this exercise especially useful at moments when you are anxious or angry.

With roots in Buddhism and the other great spiritual traditions, this is a wonderful practice for both beginners and advanced practitioners.

i. Mindfulness of Breathing

This particular version of the Mindfulness of Breathing is mainly aimed to calm and focus the mind, and is therefore what is known as a samatha (Sanskrit, shamatha), or calming practice rather than a vipassana, or insight, one.

The Sanskrit equivalent to the word vipassana is vipashyana and both words mean insight, or truly seeing the nature of reality.

The traditional name for this meditation practice is Anapanasati. This word simply means mindfulness (sati) of breathing (pana) in and out. This is a meditation practice where we use the breath as the object of attention to which we return every time we notice that the mind has wandered.

In a nutshell, this practice works mainly through us withdrawing our attention from distracting thoughts and redirecting our attention to the physical sensations of the breath. By doing so, we are putting less energy into the emotional states of restlessness, anxiety, craving, and ill will, etc that drive those thoughts.

Over time, the mind becomes calmer and our emotional states become more balanced and positive, and our experience becomes more positive.

ii. Abdominal Breathing

Most people tend to breathe in a slightly abnormal way, they tend to hold in their stomachs, make little use of their diaphragm; they breathe using the muscles of their upper chest, neck and shoulders. This is not the most effective way to get the needed oxygen to our brain and muscles.

If we watch babies or animals breathe, we will notice that they breathe with their whole bodies, their bellies rise and fall with each breath. For some reason, we stop doing this when we outgrow diapers. No one really knows why.

The good prospect is that we can relearn how to breathe properly–learning to breathe using our abdomens. This can help us control our feelings of stress. In fact, abdominal breathing is the single most effective strategy for stress reduction.

A person's normal breathing rate is 8-12 breaths per minute. However, if some one is stressed or he is under panic attack, he tends to breathe faster (up to 20-30 breaths per minute) but more shallowly. Although we may seem to be breathing more when this happens, we are not actually getting much oxygen in, and the breathing is not as effective as it could be.

Abdominal breathing means breathing fully from abdomen or from the bottom of lungs. It is exactly the reverse of the way we breathe when we are anxious or tense, which is typically shallow and high in our chest.

If one is breathing from his abdomen, he can place his hand on his abdomen and see it actually rise each time he inhales. We can experience that abdominal breathing helps us to relax any time we are feeling anxious.

4

Scientific Views of Breathing

Breathing techniques and patterns are regularly advocated for relaxation, stress management, control of psycho physiological states and to improve organ function (Ritz and Roth, 2003). Anatomically speaking there is a favorable equilibrium (balance in breathing pressures) with breathing, which can be easily disrupted by fatigue or prolonged sympathetic (excitatory) nervous system arousal as seen with stress.

One therapeutic goal of yoga is that it may reduce or alleviate some of the chronic negative effects of stress. This stress relief is one reason that breathing, or pranayama as it is called in yoga, is very central to yoga practices.

Breathing, called ventilation consists of two phases, inspiration and expiration. During inspiration the diaphragm and the external inter-costal muscles contract. The diaphragm moves downward increasing the volume of the thoracic (chest) cavity, and the external inter-costal muscles pull the ribs up and outward; this expands the rib cage and increases chest volume.

This increase of volume lowers the air pressure in the lungs as compared to atmospheric air. Because air always flows from a region of high pressure to an area of lower pressure, it travels in through the body's conducting airway (nostrils, throat, larynx and trachea) into the alveoli of the lungs. During a resting expiration the diaphragm and external inter-costal muscles relax, restoring the thoracic cavity to its original (smaller) volume, and forcing air out of the lungs into the atmosphere.

Whereas breathing is involved with the movement of air into and out of the thoracic cavity, respiration involves the exchange of gases in the lungs.

With each breath, air passes through its conducting zone into the microscopic air sacs in the lunges called alveoli. It is here that external (referring to the lungs) respiration occurs. External respiration is the exchange of oxygen and carbon dioxide between the air and the blood in the lungs. Blood enters the lungs via the pulmonary arteries. It then proceeds through arterioles and into the very tiny alveolar capillaries.

Oxygen and carbon dioxide are exchanged between the blood and the air; oxygen is loaded onto the red blood cells while carbon dioxide is unloaded from them into the air. The oxygenated blood then flows out of the alveolar capillaries, through venules, and back to the heart via the pulmonary veins. The heart then pumps the blood throughout the systemic arteries to deliver oxygen throughout the body.

The respiratory center in the brainstem is responsible for controlling a person's breathing rate. It sends a message to the respiratory muscles telling them when to breathe. The medulla, located nearest the spinal cord, directs the spinal cord to maintain breathing, and the pans, a part of the brain very near the medulla, provides further smoothing of the respiration pattern. This control is automatic, involuntary and continuous. One does not have to consciously think about it.

The respiratory center knows how to control the breathing rate and depth by the amount (or percent) of carbon dioxide, oxygen and acidosis in the arterial blood (Willmore and Costill, 2004). There are receptors, called chemo-receptors, in the arch of the aorta and throughout the arteries that send signals and feedback (to the respiratory center) to increase or decrease the ventilatory output depending on the condition of these metabolic variables.

For example, when we exercise, carbon dioxide levels increase significantly which alert the chemo-receptors, which subsequently notify the brain's respiratory center to increase the speed and depth of breathing. This elevated respiration rids the body of excess carbon dioxide and supplies the body with more oxygen, which is needed during aerobic exercise.

Upon cessation of the exercise, breathing rate and depth gradually declines until carbon dioxide in the arterial blood returns to normal levels; the respiratory center will no longer be activated, and breathing rate is restored to a pre-exercise pattern. This arterial pressure regulation feedback system that carbon dioxide, oxygen and blood acid levels provide is referred to as the metabolic control of breathing (Gallego, Nsegbe, and Durand, 2001).

Breathing is most unique as compared to other visceral (e.g. digestion, endocrine cardiovascular) functions, in that it can also be regulated voluntarily. The behavioral or voluntary control of breathing is located in the cortex of the brain and describes that aspect of breathing with conscious control, such as a self-initiated change in breathing before a vigorous exertion or effort.

Speaking, singing and playing some instruments (e.g. clarinet, flute, saxophone, trumpet, etc.) are good examples of the behavioral control of breathing and are short-lived interventions (Guz, 1997). As well, the behavioral control of breathing encompasses accommodating changes in breathing such as those changes from stress and emotional stimuli.

The differentiation between voluntary and automatic (metabolic) breathing is that automatic breathing requires no attention to maintain, whereas voluntary breathing involves a given amount of focus (Gallego, Nsegbe, and Durand, 2001). Gallego and colleagues note that it is not fully understood how the behavioral and metabolic controls of respirations are linked.

Pranayama breathing is often performed in yoga and meditation. It means the practice of voluntary breath control and refers to inhalation, retention and exhalation that can be performed quickly or slowly (Jerath et al., 2006). As such, yoga breathing is considered "an intermediary between the mind and body (Sovik, 2000)."

In many yoga stories and literature the word 'prana' (part of the word 'pranayama' for breathing) refers to the 'life force' or energy. This has many applications, especially as it relates to the energy producing processes within the body.

There is a direct connection between the 'prana' or energy of breathing and its effects on energy liberation in the body. Cellular metabolism (reactions in the cell to produce energy) for example, is regulated by oxygen provided during breathing.

The yoga purpose of breath training is not to over-ride the body's autonomic systems; although there is clear evidence that pranayama breathing techniques can effect oxygen consumption and metabolism (Jerath et al., 2006). In fact, much of the aim of pranayama breathing appears to shift the autonomic nervous system away from its sympathetic (excitatory) dominance.

Pranayama breathing has been shown to positively affect immune function, hypertension, asthma, autonomic nervous system imbalances, and psychological or stress-related disorders (Jerath et al., 2006).

Jerath and colleagues add that investigations regarding stress and psychological improvements support evidence that pranayama breathing alters the brain's information processing, making it an intervention that improves a person's psychological profile.

Sovik notes that the main philosophy behind the yoga control of breathing is to "increase awareness and understanding of the relationship between cognitive states, physical functioning, and breathing styles."

According to Sovik, breath training includes the ability to sustain relaxed attention on the flow of breath, to refine and control respiratory movements for optimal breathing, and to integrate awareness and respiratory functioning in order to reduce stress and enhance psychological functioning.

It is interesting to also recognize that there are several different types of breathing common to yoga, including the complete yoga breath (conscious breathing in the lower, middle, and upper portions of the lungs), interval breathing (in which the duration of inhalation and exhalation are altered), alternate nostril breathing, and belly breathing to name a few (Collins, 1998, Jerath et al., 2006).

It is also equally worthy to observe that breath awareness was originally developed to the movements being done by the yogi to achieve the joining of the mind, body, and spirit in search for self-awareness, health and spiritual growth (Collins). Although numerous studies show clinically beneficial health effects of pranayama-breathing.

Slow pranayama breathing techniques show the most practical and physiological benefit, yet the underlying mechanism how they work is not fully elucidated in the research (Jerath et al., 2006).

However, Jerath and colleagues hypothesize that "the voluntary, slow deep breathing functionally resets the autonomic nervous system through stretch-induced inhibitory signals and hyper-polarization (slowing electrical action potentials) currents, which synchronizes neural elements in the heart, lungs, limbic system and cortex."

As well, investigations have demonstrated that slow breathing pranayama breathing techniques activate the parasympathetic (inhibitory) nervous system, thus slowing certain physiological processes down that may be functioning too fast or conflicting with the homeostasis of the cells (Jerath et al., 2006).

In order to maintain awareness on breathing and to reduce distractions, yoga participants use comfortable postures with the eyes closed. The outcome of mastering this breath control is that an individual can voluntarily use these practices to ease stressful or discomforting situations.

Yoga participants learn how to deal with distractions and stress without having an emotionally stimulating physiological response. They practice doing this by first recognizing whatever the distraction or thought may be, and then returning or restoring the focus of attention back to breathing (Sovik, 2000).

The re-focus centers on the thoughts "I am breathing" (Sovik). Yoga enthusiasts also use 'asanas' or specific postures with pranayama breathing, linking the movement or body position with the breathing. Jerath et al. (2006) state that more research is needed to understand how the combined approach of breathing and asanas elicit beneficial health outcomes.

Although the diaphragm is one of the primary organs responsible for respiration, it is believed by some yogis to be under functioning in many people (Sovik, 2000). Thus, there is often emphasis placed upon diaphragmatic breathing, rather than the use of the overactive chest muscles.

Anatomically the diaphragm sits beneath the lungs and is above the organs of the abdomen. It is the separation between cavities of the torso (the upper or thoracic and the lower or abdominal). It is attached at the base of the ribs, the spine, and the sternum.

As describe earlier, when the diaphragm contracts the middle fibers, which are formed in a dome shape, descend into the abdomen, causing thoracic volume to increase (and pressure to fall), thus drawing air into the lungs. The practice of proper breathing techniques is aimed at eliminating misused accessory chest muscles, with more emphasis on diaphragmatic breathing.

With diaphragmatic breathing the initial focus of attention is on the expansion of the abdomen, sometimes referred to as abdominal or belly breathing. Have a client place one hand on the abdomen above the navel to feel it being pushed outward during the inhalations. Next, the breathing focus includes the expansion of the rib cage during the inhalation.

Correct diaphragmatic breathing will elicit a noticeable lateral expansion of the rib cage. Diaphragmatic breathing should be practiced in the supine, prone and erect positions, as these are the functional positions of daily life.

Finally, the diaphragmatic breathing is integrated with physical movements, asanas, during meditation and during relaxation. Analogous to the seasoned cyclist, who is able to maintain balance effortlessly while cycling, the practitioner in diaphragmatic breathing can focus attention on activities of daily life while naturally doing diaphragmatic breathing.

To summarize, Sovik suggests the characteristics of optimal breathing (at rest) are that it is diaphragmatic, nasal (inhalation and exhalation), smooth, deep, even, quiet and free of pauses.

References

Collins, C. (1998). Yoga: Intuition, preventive medicine, and treatment. Journal of Obstetric, Gynecologic, and Neonatal Nursing, 27 (5) 563-568.

Gallego, J., Nsegbe, E. and Durand, E. (2001). Learning in respiratory control. Behavior Modification, 25 (4) 495-512.

Guz, A. (1997). Brain, breathing and breathlessness. Respiration Physiology. 109, 197-204.

Jerath, R., Edry J.W, Barnes, V.A., and Jerath, V. (2006). Physiology of long pranayamic breathing: Neural respiratory elements may provide a mechanism that explains how slow deep breathing shifts the autonomic nervous system. Medical Hypothesis, 67, 566-571.

National Center for Health Statistics. (2002). U.S. Department of Health and Human Services. Centers for Disease Control and Prevention.

http://www.cdc.gov/nchs/products/pubs/pubd/hestats/asthma/asthma.htm

Pal, G.K. Velkumary, S. and Madanmohan. (2004). Effect of short-term practice of breathing exercises on autonomic functions in normal human volunteers. Indian Journal of Medical Research, 120, 115-121.

Repich, D. (2002). Overcoming concerns about breathing. National Institute of Anxiety and Stress, Inc.

Ritz, T. and Roth, W.T. (2003). Behavioral intervention in asthma. Behavior Modification. 27 (5), 710-730.

Sovik, R. (2000). The science of breathing – The yogic view. Progress in Brain Research, 122 (Chapter 34), 491-505.

Willmore, J. and Costill, D. (2004). Physiology of Sport and Exercise (3rd Edition). Champaign: Human Kinetics.

i. Breathe Secret

Correct breathing has become extremely challenging in modern society. The process of breathing has been warped by chronic stress, sedentary life-styles, unhealthy diets and lack of fitness. All of these contribute to poor breathing habits. These in turn contribute to lethargy, weight gain, sleeping problems, respiratory conditions, and heart diseases.

Modern living gradually increases the amount of air we breathe, and while getting more oxygen into our lungs might seem like a good idea, it is in fact light breathing that is a testament to good health and fitness.

The biggest obstacle to our heath and fitness is rarely identified problem i.e. chronic over breathing. We breathe two to three times more air than required without knowing it.

Over breathing causes the narrowing of airways, limiting your body's ability to oxygenate and the constriction of blood vessels, leading to reduced blood flow to heart and other organs and muscles.

Role of Oxygen and Carbon Dioxide in Breathing Process

The amount of oxygen our muscles, organs, and tissues are able to use is not entirely depended on the amount of oxygen in our blood. Our red blood cells are saturated with maximum of 99 percent oxygen.

It must be understood that amount of oxygen used actually by our body depends on amount of carbon dioxide in our blood. We know from basic science of biology that we breathe in oxygen and breathe out carbon dioxide. This carbon dioxide is the key variable that allows the release of oxygen from the red blood cells to be metabolized by the body. This is called the Bohr Effect.

It must be understood that when we breathe correctly, we have sufficient amount of carbon dioxide, and our breathing is quite, controlled, and rhythmic. If we are over breathing, our breathing is heavy, more intense, and erratic, and we exhale too much carbon dioxide, leaving our body literally gasping for oxygen.

In fact, if we breathe better, increasing the amount of carbon dioxide inside us, we deliver more oxygen to our muscles and organs, including heart and brain, and thus we heighten our physical capacity.

Furthermore, at high altitude i.e. at mountains, the air is thin, which results in reduced atmospheric pressure of oxygen. The body adapts to this environment by increasing the number of red blood cells. Increasing the presence of red blood cells leads into improved oxygen delivery to the muscles. This enhances better overall performance including longer endurance.

Human Respiratory System

Our respiratory system comprises the parts of body that delivers oxygen from atmosphere to our cells and tissues and transport the carbon dioxide produced in tissues back into the atmosphere.

When we breathe, air enters the body and flows down the windpipe (trachea), which the divides into two branches called bronchi: One branch lead to right lung, the other to the left. Within lungs, the bronchi further subdivide into smaller branches called bronchioles, and eventually into a multitude of small air sacs called alveoli. Alveoli transport oxygen into the blood.

The lungs contain approximately 30 Lakhs (300 million) of alveoli, each of which is surrounded by tiny blood vessels called capillaries. The contact surface between alveoli and blood capillary is quite large that provides the potential for an extremely efficient transfer of oxygen to the blood.

Oxygen is the fuel that muscles need to work efficiently. It is, however, a common misconception that breathing in a large volume of air increases the oxygenation of the blood. It is physiologically impossible to increase the oxygen saturation of the blood in this way, because the blood is always almost fully saturated. It is the percentage of red blood cells (hemoglobin molecules) containing oxygen within the blood.

During the periods of rest the standard breathing volume for a healthy person is between 4 and 6 liters of air per minute, which results in almost complete oxygen saturation of 95 to 99 percent.

Because oxygen is continually diffusing from blood into the cells, 100 percent saturation is not always feasible. An oxygen saturation of 100 percent would suggest that bond between red blood cells and oxygen molecules are too strong, reducing the blood cell's ability to deliver oxygen to muscles, organs and tissues. Basically, it is needed the blood to release oxygen, not to hold on it.

Regulation of Breathing

There are two main aspects to the way we breathe: the rate or number of breaths per minute and the volume or amount of air drawn into lungs with each breath. Although the two are separate, one generally influences the other. A healthy person takes 10 to 12 breaths per minute drawing in a volume of 500 milliliters of air, for a total volume of 5 to 6 liters. If a person is breathing at a higher rate—at 20 breaths per minute, then volume will also be higher.

In short, it must be understood that it is not oxygen that exerts the primary influence on your breathing efficiency, but carbon dioxide.

The crucial point to remember is that hemoglobin releases oxygen when in the presence of carbon dioxide. When we over breathe, too much carbon dioxide is washed from lungs, blood, tissues, and cells. This condition is called hypocapnia, causing the hemoglobin to hold on to oxygen, resulting in reduced oxygen release and therefore reduced oxygen delivery to tissues and organs. With less oxygen delivered, organs, muscles and brain will become lethargic.

Moreover, too much breathing can cause reduced blood flow. Heavy breathing even for short interval is enough to reduce blood circulation throughout the body, including brain, which can cause a feeling of dizziness and light-headedness. In general, blood flow to the brain reduces proportionately to each reduction in carbon dioxide.

pH of Blood and Carbon dioxide

In addition, carbon dioxide plays a central role in regulating the pH of the bloodstream: how acidic or alkaline is blood. Normal pH in the blood is 7.365. When this level increases, breathing reduces. Conversely, if the pH of the blood is too acidic (when more processed acidic food is consumed), breathing increases in order to offload carbon dioxide as acid, allowing pH to normalize. pH level affects the metabolism of the body.

Also, over breathing causes carbon dioxide levels to drop, less oxygen will be delivered to muscles and organs.

Nose Breathing and Nitric Oxide

It is surprised to know that nose is a great source for Nitric Acid. Nasal breathing is imperative for harnessing the benefits of nitric oxide, working hand in hand with abdominal breathing and helping to maximize body oxygenation. Each time we breathe gently and slowly through the nose, we carry this mighty molecule into lungs and blood, where it can work throughout the body.

Nitric oxide plays an important role in vasoregulation (the opening and closing of blood vessels), homeostasis (the way in which the body maintain a state of stable physiological balance in order to stay alive), neurotransmission (the messaging system within the brain), immune defense, and respiration. It helps to prevent high blood pressure, lower cholesterol, keep the arteries young and flexible, and prevent the clogging of arteries with Plaque and clots. All these reduce the risk of heart attack and stroke.

ii. Science of Breathing Behind Samadhi/Mergence

Nirvikalpa and Savikalpa Samadhi/mergence occur, as we know, when some one transcends time and space; when his consciousness is merged with the Supernal. What happens under this condition? What transformations occur to his physical body, mind and consciousness in this ultimate achievement in life? It is mystery of mysteries.

In this stage aspirant is in conscious-less state, mind is annihilated, however, exactly no one can say what transformations have taken place. What little known is that mind becomes thought-less: there remains no awareness of any kind in moments of Savikalpa Samadhi; however, awareness is discontinuous; it comes and goes? One is in void so he can not express what happens; he awakes with manifested consciousness but without any glimpses of that stage, when he was merged or he had passed through or what he experienced in that stage.

On the contrary, if he enters in Nirvikalpa Samadhi, then he never comes back in human consciousness; it is like merging of drop of water in ocean loosing its identity. Drop of water and ocean water become the same. This happens at the stage of death.

What happens to physical body in the Savikalpa Samadhi? This has been tempted to diagnose in the light of present day advancement of science. This may be explained reviewing the inner physiological condition of the body in the moments of mergence; and also, perceiving the changes experienced in the physical body immediately after the consciousness re-appeared.

We all well know that during meditation, one is introvert; he is aware of what so ever is going inside in his mind. He is aware of his multiple series of thoughts. As he witnesses his own thoughts in meditation, frequency of appearance of thoughts is reduced.

There are as many as 112 techniques of meditation. One can follow any technique based on his temperament; all means and ways finally take him to the door of mergence after years of long practice. However, every technique moves around breathing process, breathing pattern and so on. Breath is only the medium, which communicates with internal and external world around;

breath only takes consciousness to skywards; it takes to the stage of mergence.

In meditation, finally one visualizes the inner life force energy that moves in the system, which gets establish in Ajana chakra after years of practice; and then it takes pathless path as divine light and travels upwards towards apex centre passing through nine dormant chakras of Chida Akasha through Unmani Chakra existing close to Sahasara Chakra.

Different chapters of the book discuss the evolution of Life force energy and its movement from Muladhara Chakra onwards. Here we will be discussing how the breathing science physiologically plays a vital role in achievement of self -realization and mergence; and how the breathing process helps appearance of life force; and subsequently how life force is manifested in the physical body by proper and controlled breathing practices.

In the process of meditation, when one observes his breath with full awareness i.e. when he observes closely breath in and breath out; gradually he experiences that number of breaths in and out per minutes gets reduced. For a normal person taking approximately 10 to 15 breaths per minute, gradually they are reduced to 4 and even less in course of meditation when he gets deeply engrossed.

He can easily perceive that breath becomes very light and intake of air in a single breath is also reduced. As the frequency of breath is reduced, the time span between two consecutive breaths in and out is increased; it means discontinuity between two consecutive breath increases i.e. time gap increases when there is no breath inside till the fresh breath comes.

In the above process there is more carbon dioxide in the system since fresh breath has not entered and existing inside breath has not left. Thus, level of carbon dioxide increases in the system. Since a human being breath out carbon dioxide and breath intake is mostly oxygen along with other in-gradients from out side atmosphere.

In these moments of natural breath less state i.e. in discontinuity between two consecutive breaths i.e. in take and exist; in presence of excess carbon dioxide in the system that forces to release more oxygen from blood to physical organs, to heart and to brain; this give more energy to overall physical system to make it more healthier.

As meditation goes deeper and deeper, breath rate further reduces and excess carbon dioxide is piled up in the system; and thus heart, brain and body organs get surplus energy by getting more oxygen from blood. This is because of fact in discontinuity, carbon dioxide level increases and more oxygen gets absorbed into the system.

Moreover in meditation, there is no physical movement of any kind, heart rate is reduced; all the senses are introvert and eyes are closed; this leads to further enhance energy level in the system along with excessive flow of oxygen from the blood.

It must be known that most of human energy is utilized in general living and routine work by eyes, lungs and heart beats etc. Since the complete system is under restful condition during meditation so major organs is not able to use sufficient energy, so surplus unused energy is available in the system.

This excessive energy is transformed into life force energy in association with "Shavasa"—the breath and its level is manifested multifold in the system. This adds to already available pranic energy, transformed from the routine breathing process.

Thus, overall life force/pranic energy is increased in the system that strengthens the body and makes the body healthy inwardly. Also, this surplus life force energy can travel though the human nerves/nadis/system having least resistance.

Gradually as the meditation is continued, the body becomes saturated of this fine energy. Since mind is introvert and is kept closely associated with the spinal cord by yogic practices, so it gets saturated with excess life force energy; and then life force energy can travel easily through very fine Sushumana nadi located in between ida and pingala nadis of spinal cord through Muladhara, if directed mentally by deep meditation yoga practices.

As per Paramhansa Yogananda, one round of travel of life force to Ajna chakra and back is equivalent to one year of evolution of a human being by proper living and engrossment in divinity.

Life force energy is basically Pranic energy—the Chi energy. One can experience this energy in short time span by yogic practices particularly by Kriya yoga practices, which is very fine, sacred art of breathing. This is revealed and taught by ancient masters. By silence of mind and through secret art of breathing by regulating breathing, life force energy—the divine energy can be enhanced. All this is feasible by the grace and blessing of unknown divine force. However, techniques and methods do accelerate the process.

Life force energy can also be enhanced by creating vacuum in the system i.e. by exhausting out air in side the system gradually. This is possible by less breath in take i.e. to take breath in take for short duration and more exhausts of air from the system through nostril for sufficiently long duration. This process reduces the gases in side the body since intake of air is gradually reducing. As this process is continued vacuum of air will be experienced in the system.

During these moments, more oxygen will be released by blood and absorbed by the system by the available level of carbon dioxide present in the system. This will generate abundance of life force in the system and can be easily experienced after regular practice.

This leads to enhance health, happiness and well-being. This makes easy to transcendence of time and space with availability of surplus life force. This acts as a very useful tool to succeed in deep meditation to take life force energy to apex centre to be in the Savikalpa Samadhi.

Also, recitation of AUM mantra by the proper breathing technique is very helpful to easily reach the stage of mergence. It is possible if 'M' of AUM is prolonged much longer as compared to "A" and "U" during recitation such that air inside is made to exit from the system and gradually vacuums is created and experienced in side the system. By this process inside gases are breathed out and fresh air is not entered.

This condition too generates excess life force by absorption of oxygen form blood by system organs through remaining carbon dioxide in the system. Basically, this too is by secret of breath though recitation of AUM japa in a proper scientific way by complete awareness.

All above pattern and ways of breathings reduce number of breaths per minute. In this way life force energy is increased by slow breathing process and increase of carbon dioxide leads to enhance oxygen levels in physical system, which finally leads to increase pH level of inner system. Increased pH level leads to less breathe per minute since more oxygen is released from hemoglobin of the blood. Under these conditions, system does not need more oxygen so the breath rate reduces by feed back control automatically. This makes human system healthily, strong and disease free.

Moreover, taking breath through nostrils, nitric oxide of air is absorbed in nostrils that further strengthens the immune system, controls blood pressure and take care of overall well being of the physical system.

As life force transcends through Muladhara Chakra along with Kundilini power through Sushumna nadi of spinal cord in deep meditation, breath rate is automatically and gradually reduced. It turns to be 1 to 2 breaths per minutes. By this body energy and excessive oxygen in the body and vitality increases and aspirant can comfortably sit in timeless zone focusing all his energy within himself. Thus, at Ajana Chakra–the place between eye brows, at third eye location, mind, soul, consciousness and life force turn into as combined unit of divine energy.

Furthermore, breath rate at this stage become minimal and gap i.e. discontinuity between two consecutive breaths in and out increases; this is gradual approaching stage of breath suspension. As breathe suspension is continued, combined unit divine energy moves skyward through Unmani Chakra to Sahasara towards Apex centre. However, aspirant is in wakefulness with discontinuity; some time partially he is awake and sometime he is in conscious-less stage. This is continued; he experiences the presence of feeble breath with more discontinuity.

After some time, a stage comes when breath is completely suspended; combined unit divine energy i.e. consciousness through apex centre merges with the Supernal–the Universal consciousness as divine light; then no breath, no awareness for a few moments is experienced; this is the stage of divine romance. After this gap of discontinuity when continuity re-appears, feeling of breath, mind and consciousness is gradually restored.

In fact before final divine romance, unit consciousness passes through awakening, slum state of partial awakening, dreamless state and gradually to conscious-less state of final mergence. This is the state of oneness without any feeling of breath; one is with the Almighty; he and He, the Almighty, become one.

One comes back from this stage with immense peace, expanded consciousness experiencing as if he has gone in different universe where there was no breath, no consciousness; he was in Nirvikalpa Samadhi. This is unique experience that comes by grace and blessing of Almighty. This experience can be repeated by the blessing of God. Nothing more is as unique, pleasant and miraculous as this.

This is miracle and secret of sacred breath; with out breath this experience is not feasible. Breath is the Master. Only through breath mergence is feasible.

5

Chi Energy and Breathing

Chi (sometimes spelled Qi) is vital energy and it is closely related to breathing.

Broad concept of Chi energy is world wide adequately known. Chi refers to the natural energy of the Universe, which permeates everything. All matter, from the smallest atoms and molecules to the largest planets and stars, is made up of this energy. It is the vital force of life. It is the source of every existing thing.

Chi has many manifestations. To the kung fu and taiji practitioners of China it is known as "Chi," but different philosophies and cultures call it by different names. Japanese martial arts call it "Ki." Metaphysical science calls it "vital force." Friedrich Mesmer called it "animal magnetism." The Indian and Hindu yogis call it "Prana." Western science defines it as "biorhythm," and New Age thinkers simply call it "cosmic energy."

Naturally, in each manifestation the Chi is viewed and defined differently, but basically it is the same thing. It is the power which enables us to think, move, breathe, and live – the power that makes gravity act like gravity. It is what makes electricity electric. It is the link between our perception of the inner and outer worlds.

It is our connection to the very flow of the universe and the prime moving force within a human body. Chi is not breath; it is the power that makes it possible for us to breathe. Chi is not simply "energy," it is what gives energy the power to be energy. Chi is the power behind movement and thought...and it is everywhere. It is in the oxygen we breathe and the blood that flows through us.

It is difficult to define Chi concretely. It cannot be seen; it can not be measured; it cannot be touched or captured. It is everywhere, yet we have no way to touch it, make it tangible, or even prove its existence. Therefore Chi is a difficult concept to accept.

The Western mind likes the tangible, the concrete and the specific. It likes a scientific explanation, which defines, dissects, and categorizes. Chi transcends this kind of explanation. It doesn't fit easily into a strict biomedical framework. It is simply indefinable in those terms.

Chi within the body is like power in a rechargeable battery. Occasionally it needs to be replenished. The Chi of the universe is inexhaustible, yet the body needs fresh Chi to maintain its vitality. When we are exchanging the Chi within us with the Chi of the universe, we feel healthy and vigorous.

By energizing the body with Chi it is revitalized naturally, enabling it to fight off illness and maintain good health. The true secret to replenishing Chi resides in our breathing.

Breathing in and out through the nose is the only method that enables the body to process Chi energy effectively. Most people understand the importance of breathing in through the nose. When we breathe in through the nose, there are a series of defence mechanisms that prevent impurities, and extremely cold air from entering in the body.

First, a screen of nose hairs traps dust and other particles that could injure the lungs if we breathe through the mouth. Next, there is a long passage lined with mucus membranes, where excessively cool air is warmed and very fine dust particles that escaped the hair screen are caught.

Finally, in the inner nose are glands which fight off bacteria that may have slipped through the other defences. The inner nose also contains the olfactory organ that gives us our sense of smell, which can detect poisonous fumes that could damage our health if we were to breathe them.

Breathing through the nose requires a deeper understanding of the nature of Chi energy. Practitioners of martial arts, especially karate, need to absorb and process the Chi that they are breathing in order to generate the power and force for the techniques they practice.

They also need to be able to retain the Chi within the body until the moment it is needed. Basically, when we inhale, we are bringing fresh oxygen and Chi into our body. When we exhale through the mouth, we are expelling carbon dioxide, which contains all the toxins and poisons that have built up within the lungs.

We are also expelling Chi from the body. But if we are continuously expelling the Chi, we never give it a chance build up into the rich source of energy needed to complete our techniques to their maximum effectiveness. By exhaling through the mouth, we simply allow the Chi energy to dissipate back into the world.

Breathing through the nose, however, completes a closed circuit. By exhaling through the nose, rather than allowing the Chi energy to be expelled with the carbon dioxide, we transfer it to the dan tien or hara, located about three finger widths below the umbilicus.

With each breath we take in, more Chi enters the body and circles down to the dan tien, growing stronger and stronger. During this breathing process, the tongue is up, touching the top palate of the mouth just behind the front teeth and the air is expelled from the nose with a slightly audible hiss. There is also a feeling of the abdominal walls contracting down with the exhalation.

Once sufficient Chi has been generated this way, the practitioner is able to direct the Chi with tremendous force. Remember that Chi is a subtle, invisible force that requires much patience and long years of practice to understand. The ability to relax and breathe effectively will benefit in building Chi.

When our mind and body are working together in a relaxed manner and we are breathing properly, a tremendous amount of energy is able to flow through us. The key is not to force it, just slow down, relax and breathe through the nose.

6
Breath is Life

Guru Nanak in the Epilogue of Japuji Sahib of Guru Granth Sahib has very clearly brought out the importance of breath in human life. As per Guru Nanak breath is life and one cannot survive without breath even for a nano second. As per Him breath is a ladder to reach the ultimate; it is way of realization; it is master; guide and path of mergence with ultimate.

This epilogue has been brought out below with explanation to justify the unlimited abundance blessing of breath in human life.

Sloka - The Epilogue (From Japu Ji Sahib of Guru Granth Sahib) *

Pavan Guru Pani Pita Mata Dharti Mahat

Divas Raat Doye Daee Daya Khele Sagar Jatat

Changiyanian Buriyanian Vache Dharam Hadoor

Karma Aapo Apani Ke Nere Ke Door

Jini Naam Dhiayia Gae Masakat Ghaal

Nanak Te Mukh Ujale Keti Chutti Naal

Explanation

In this epilogue, Guru Nanak Ji has expressed the philosophy of existence of a human being in very simple and impressive words. In simple straight words it is said that air/breath is Guru/the master, water is father and earth is the great mother. The day and nights are nurses in whose lap the world plays. The mysterious and deeper meaning of this Sloka is quite difficult to express. However, it can be said that without food, one can live for a few days, without water for couple of hours but without air one cannot live even for a microsecond.

Without breathe, there is no life. Breathing process goes on automatically where as one needs to consume food and drink water by self-efforts. So air, which a creature consumes constantly, is the master, the Guru, and without the guidance and direction of Guru, the light, the existence, the life ceases. So, the air is regarded as Guru.

Furthermore, air is woven with the Prana; the life force, which is the sole part of existence. A human being is declared dead when life force/soul/consciousness leaves a physical body. Life force is the instrument for functioning of all the vital elements of the system for movement of the cycle of life. So, the air is called the master/ Guru, which is the gateway to the Almighty.

If one can experience the life force mentally in his physical body and can monitor it by the grace of God, he can climb the ladder of self-realization by the blessings of Almighty. This is basic prerequisite of spiritual development. That is the reason, air i.e. breath is Guru/master and by its assistance, one can merge in Almighty and realizes Him.

Water is like the father since one third of universe is water; and our body has one-third by volume water only. Water transmits coolness; and cleans, maintains our system. Most of human works/ activities go around water only. There is no life without water. Water is the nucleus of human life for all his activities. Without father there is no creation and so without water, there is no existence/life.

Mother earth acts like a live real mother in our life. She, the mother earth, grows food to feeds us. Take care of our excreta, dissolve in her and still maintains her beauty and maintains her surroundings. Mother earth is supreme in all respects to get our life moving smoothly. One gets education from mother, father and master/Guru. The fellow is blessed if he gets supreme mother, father and master, so that he gets proper virtues and wisdom and the supreme knowledge of God's realization.

Furthermore, air cannot be controlled in the boundaries. It is formless like Almighty; it is like cosmic light that guides the human being. It is supernal, the guide to our soul. Water is like mind in a human being. It can go any where by changing its form. It is forceful entity. Earth mother is like physical body and takes care of our basic physical needs.

In fact, body is mother earth, water is mind and soul is the air .All physical being have body, human being have mind of various levels of development and only spiritually evolved human being have evolved soul/consciousness that can merge in air/the Pranic light, the supernal.

The play of day and night in this universe is for our safety, joy and nourishment. Day and night are the representative of the time, and by their presence this worldly play is going on by the process of relishing the energy and using it as needed. If one transcendences time, merges self in the zone of timeless; he becomes liberated and then only he is self realized.

In the span of lifetime, a human being does all type of actions. Out of all his actions, some of them are good and some actions are not good; not healthier; these might be sinful; these might be executed intentionally or might have been done unintentionally. The lord of justices' watches all good and bad deeds.

Every action is judged based on its merit. If one is pure, he will be near to God. One can execute no sinful action if he is nearer to the God. If the actions executed by some one are not good, and are sinful, this indicates that Almighty does not bless him. Divine virtues are far away from him.

In other words some action draw closeness to Him and other actions shall further recede him from Almighty. However, God is stable under all conditions. Only individual actions change his location with respect to Almighty.

What one reaps that he gets. All fruits to an individual are the resultant of his right and wrong actions. So, one need not to blame others for troubles and miseries of own life. One him self is responsible for all his troubles. This must be very clearly understood and well conceived.

Almighty is like fire. Whosoever is near to Him; get his warmth; and it holds well by the Almighty. More one is closer to Almighty; he is showered more of His blessings. But at the same time Almighty is kind to His devotees, likes and favors the lovable devotees and also, He is the perfect judge for them.

Those, who merge in the glory of Almighty, mediate on Him; He dissolves all miseries of such devotional devotees. Such devotees are perfect in their austerities. In fact such devotees don't have any desire and they don't demand any thing from Almighty. They are desire-less and all their activities are selfless. All miseries of life, they consider the divine gift from Almighty. Those who are merged in His glory, their faces are graceful; their actions, their company, their deeds are praise worthy. Even company of such people liberates the fellow being.

In general, those who meditate are able to sublimate their toil. Guru Nanak Ji says, such people have effulgent bright/graceful faces, and they are able to redeem many others with their strides.

*(From the book *"Unison at Core"* published by Lap Academic Publications, Germany, 2012; authored by Dr. Har Prashad).

Also

*(From the book *"Japu Ji Sahib and Srimad Bhagavad-Gita—The Spark of Enlightenment"* published by Books For All (an Imprint of Low Price Publications, Delhi, India), 2011; authored by Dr. Har Prashad)

7

Role of Breath in Transcendence and Well-Being

In a human system there are two basic Nadis connected with the two nostrils. Surya Nadi is connected with the right nostril, and Chandra/moon Nadi with the left nostril. Surya Nadi is atmic/soul Nadi; it is helpful to enhance divine qualities of the aspirant if it is opened; and one breathes freely through the right nostril. This is governed by left hemisphere of the brain.

Moon Nadi is Jeeva Nadi; it is helpful for better living. While freely breathing through this Nadi all sensory perceptions and emotional attitudes of the Sadhaka/aspirant are strengthened. Thus, breathing through left nostril enhances worldly perceptions; and thus one is governed more by mind. This is governed by right hemisphere of the brain.

However, if both the nostrils are opened and one breathes in and breathes out through them, then Jeeva/living being executes all his activities with complete consciousness, unison with self and homogeneity. All the noble activities are accomplished being in this state.

Breathe in this pattern, when both the nostrils are opened, is nothing but a tranquil breath; this tranquil breath flows through the Brahma Nadi that is closely associated with the Surya Nadi as well with the Moon Nadi; and it is only possible when one steps into "Being", and transcendences time & space with discontinuities.

The horizontal materialistic worldly activities of Jeeva/living being are linked with mental emotions, and are governed by the Muladhara chakra under the influence of breath when left nostril operates. Right hemisphere of the brain controls this.

Where as divine universal activities of Atma/soul are governed by Dhahara/heart chakra; when right nostril operates; and the influence of pure consciousness, soul/Atma, is predominant on the aspirant. Left hemisphere of the brain controls this. Dhahara chakra is considered as the location of the soul of living being; where Jeevatma i.e. personalized soul resides at peace.

When left nostril operates, it shows that a living being is in conscious state; he is under the influence of Maya/illusion. On the contrary when right nostril operates, it indicates that a living being is in Atmic/divine state; and he is generally unconscious/unaware of the worldly mundane activities.

However, mind is mutative and thoughts of the mind go on changing with time depending on whether a living being breathes from left nostril or right nostril. Some time he may behave like a saint, and on another occasion his thoughts are governed by the animal instinct.

If one is conscious of his mental state, he can modulate his thoughts by changing the breath pattern on altering the free flow of the air from one side of the nostril to the other side. Great Rishis/saints can change their breath pattern by their will. Such advanced Rishis/saints have symptoms of SAM YAMI LAKSHANA for controlling their thought pattern. This whole science is the science of tranquil breath.

Tranquil breath is basically variant constant and not the constant- constant; it means tranquil breath is governed by discontinuities in the continuum of breathe cycles. Disturbing thoughts can be controlled by changing the breath pattern by switching on left nostril breathing to the right nostril breathing. This is the yoga. This yoga is called CHIT VRITI NRODHA that means one changes his emotional heart feeling and thought pattern as per his own will and requirement.

Tranquil breath is most significant; and it is specifically known as divine breath. Its appearance and disappearance depends on the divine power; discontinuity is it's built in characteristics; it is not under the control of a human being. However, by modulation of physical conditions, and mental thinking and change in system vibrations, the tranquil breath can be established for a short duration. But, its longevity cannot be guaranteed.

Kula charkas, i.e. charkas below Manipura namely Muladhara and Swadhisthanam have gravitation pull, and these chakras do not allow the upward journey of Udana Prana with Kundalini power, and pull it back to the original mooring. But, once the Manipura chakra is crossed then the effect of gravitational pull of Kula Chakras seizes to exist.

In Kula chakra there is no awareness of Sakshi Chaitanya and Atam-sakshatkara/ God realization; and it is not possible unless and until the transcendence of Kula chakra is achieved, and life force reaches to Dhahara/Anahata chakra.

Udana Prana is the life force at Muladhara, Swadhisthanam and Manipura chakras; however, at Dhahara/ Anahata chakra there is a light of pure soul. This light of soul is self-abnegated at the Dhahara chakra. Jeeva/living being coupled with soul/Atma is located at this chakra as Jeevatma/ personalized soul of living being. However, Kundalini is the sleeping force at the Kula chakra, precisely at the Muladhara. Atma/soul light is in the dormant state entangled with Jeeva/living being at the Dharara chakra/ heart center.

Jeeva/human being is unconscious and is in the unmanifested stage of awareness when Kundalini power and soul are in Samadhi/ rest/being state at their respective locations/roots. Both remain in Samadhi/sleeping state unless the Pranic forces do not awaken them. After the awakening of Kundalini power and ascent of soul to the higher centers, microcosm is merged with the macrocosm, and super conscious state is achieved.

When the Kundalini power is awakened and soul ascends, the existing conscious/ aware state of the Sadhaka/aspirant turns to mergence/Laya/conscious-less state with discontinuities, and only then he enjoys the blessings of "Being". After mergence, when soul returns, its normal conscious state gets manifested.

The soul coupled/entangled with Jeeva termed as Jeevatma i.e. personalized soul; and it is the part of Shiva resting at the Dhahara/Anahata chakra. Kundalini being feminine power/Shakti, rests at Muladhara chakra. Both are merged in illusion/Maya; and are in the gross aware state of complete rest under the influence of Maya. However, when the favourable condition is created by the effect of Udana Prana; Kundilini Shakti/power gets awakened; and merges with Shiva at the Dhahara chakra; and then ascends to the Apex center through Ajna chakra.

As they merge, they become unaware of the mergence, they transform from conscious to conscious-less state with discontinuities; and become spirit power of being; then only the Sadhaka/aspirant gains the spiritual power; he steps into "Being", to be beyond time & space.

In fact, by the ascendance of this Shiv-Shakti after mergence at Anahata Chakra to Visuddhi Chakra to Lambika Chakra, this gets purified at the Ajna Chakra; Jeeva then shades the effect of mind gradually; mind is then annihilated with discontinuities; and soul/pure light gets united with the cause of creation; the supernal; the "Being"; here soul is separated from Jeeva/living being; and there is no more existence of Jeevatma as identity.

Under these conditions effect of mind disappears instantaneously; this causes the Jeeva/living being to be liberated. Soul, which was in intensive conscious state, is transformed to conscious-less being. Here at this location Jeeva and soul (Atma) are separated; and are in face to face as soul/Atma and Jeeva.

Here from this location onwards soul takes further journey to Unmani chakra in the Chidakasha after getting transformed into the divine light. The Pratyagatma, both soul and Jeeva face to face i.e. Jeevatma i.e. personalized soul split as Jeeva and Atma/soul, is the first step of evolution of the spiritual aspirant to the spirituality at the Ajna chakra.

Dyana/meditation follows yoga; nothing is better than meditation. One must meditate when breath is tranquil. To make it tranquil one can open the closed nostril by closing the open nostril, and breaths only through closed nostril forcefully. Doing this for one cycle or 9 times or two cycles of 9 times each, the closed nostril can be opened; and thus, one can establish the tranquil breath that is likely to make him peaceful in many respects. Tranquil breath is generated by itself.

Udana Prana helps the Sadhaka to be in meditation without much of self-effort. After 5 cycles of horizontal breath, automatically 6th cycle is of tranquil breath to calm down the human system. This changes the attitude of a human being towards life, and frequency of breath is reduced. This finally results in increasing the life span. Tranquil breath is bliss. It is also known as SAMYAMI SADHANA. Moreover, tranquil breath gives light; it gives health and well being besides longevity of life.

For well-being, health, happiness, longevity of life one must establish tranquil breathe in the system before meditation; this will help to go in to deep - meditation to derive the maximum benefit to evolve the self; also, this will assist him to transcendence of time and space to manifest the consciousness.

8

Breath–A Tool to Control Mind

It is very complex to understand mind since it is like perceiving of self by the self. There is no available literature, which discusses inbuilt of mind; its location in the human system; however, ways and means to control the mind have been discussed in details. In fact, mind is a great mystery; to direct the activities of mind is a most difficult and complex proposition. Mysterious and sensible aspect of mind control has not been understood so far. Control of mind is like trying to control the wind without adequate boundaries.

One can suppress his mind temporarily, make it sleepy and functionless by the help of tranquilizers, but to active/genuine control is the most difficult activity of the human race from time immemorial. Self control is the mind control; and key to mind control lies in the control of senses. It is said that one who has controlled his mind, has conquered the world.

Before going in details of various aspects of mind control, its function and its location in the human body, let us first try to understand the verbal, word and each letter meaning of the word "mind". In the word 'mind': 'm' stands for 'Maya'—the illusion, "i" stands for 'indulgence', "n" stands for 'noise', and 'd' stands for 'diversion' and 'distress'. So, literally meaning of the mind can be expressed as:

"That sensitive device of causal body of human system, which indulges in Maya/illusion through the senses by getting engaged in time bound activities that create noise in the process, and disturbances on accomplishment; the diversion and distribution of which finally results in distress".

Mind is Maya/illusion; Maya/illusion are mind. Maya is part of Brahma/the creator, so Maya is very powerful like Brahma; it cannot be controlled by any human designed means and ways. So, the mind, being the part of Maya, is a very powerful device, which is capable of creating a great distress of such a high magnitude that can completely deteriorate the human system, and make it functionless. However, mind is also capable of giving immense pleasure and happiness, which is always time bound and temporary.

By various existing universal means, it cannot be temporarily controlled; however, various means of medication and psychotherapy can suppress the mind or make it temporarily withdrawn, and transform it to functionless state. This may be the effect of brain on mind and energy taken from mind by the physical system.

However, as soon as the effect of drugs and hypnosis cease or wear-off, mind has the capability to draw more energy from the system, which can make him more and more violent, stronger and more rejuvenated than ever; and it becomes difficult to control it subsequently by all mundane means.

By medicines/drugs, in fact, it becomes more vulnerable and difficult to control with time. In deed mind is capable of holding immense energy; mind is a part of human consciousness.

So, what is to be done to control the mind? This needs to be very clearly understood and practiced. Since mind being Maya/illusion, is a part of Brahma/the creator. Hence, it is very clear that a human being with his limited capacity and capability cannot control Brahma/the creator of the universe. Thus, it becomes vivid that by any horizontal worldly means mind i.e. Maya/Brahma, cannot be controlled. It can only be temporarily suppressed.

Subsequently, if some body really wants to control the mind by sincere and honest efforts after understanding real monkey nature of the mind, then he needs to follow vertical divine path in place of horizontal worldly path. This will have double benefit, firstly the mind will get controlled since the mental energy will be utilized for vertical divine travel, and secondly the mind will get merged in the soul/consciousness losing its individuality; since soul as pure light adopts the pathless path to the Supernal/super-consciousness.

In other words, scientifically, mind/Maya/illusion/Brahma/creator is part of consciousness. Soul, the pure divine light is the core consciousness. As human consciousness/awareness gradually increases/manifested, mental potential increases; its kinetic energy is calm down; relative silence of mind is enhanced.

When by increase/manifestation of consciousness/awareness gradually gets transformed in conscious-less state with discontinuities in the deep state of meditation; then mind with relative silence is annihilated through such manifestation of consciousness; kinetic energy of the mind is diminished temporarily and absolute silence appears spontaneously.

By this, then consciousness steps in time-less zone, time disappears and stage to step in to "Being" beyond time & space appears with discontinuities. This stage completely controls the mind; and partial absolute silence is experienced when conscious state reappears after mergence with the Supernal.

Thus, with this frequent transformation of conscious state into conscious-less state in Supernal and back as the state of on/off condition of manifested conscious state in this transient period, gradually controls the mind.

The spiritual science of mind control requires an understanding of the unstable, illusive and dynamic nature of the mind. Mind takes energy for its dynamic activities from the food apart from the breath. So, to control the mind on the physical horizontal plane, it is required that food must be consumed in regulated selectively and controlled manners and breath must be fully under control.

Precisely speaking, food must be pure and Satvik so that mind must get only Satvik and pure energy, and not the Tamasik and Rajasik energies from pungent, putrid, violent — non-vegetarian food. Satvik vegetarian food gradually increases Sato-Guna and keeps the mind cool, pure and with much less of irritation. Animal like ferocious tendencies of the mind get subsided and in turn it helps the mind to be at rest, and gets awareness easily.

Not only the gross food but the food, one takes from other senses i.e. from eyes, ears, nose, tongue and skin must be pleasing and pure; it means our senses must intake Satvik vibrations i.e. we must see good in all, hear/listen good spiritual topics, smell good/fragrant items such as flowers, and be in contact with the good, pure, Satvik and divine people. Directly and indirectly these activities will help the mind to control the senses easily, and in turn mind will be under the control of self.

By pure manifested awareness and having vigilance on mind, all negative tendencies will cease to influence the mind gradually. Forceful control of mind not to be practiced; this will make the mind rebellion. Awareness is the best approach to dilute the built in tendencies of mind.

Apart from senses and food, mind gets subtle energy from breath. In fact mind requires energy from the breath at all times in order to exist. Mind becomes functionless if a human being becomes breathless. If the breath is controlled, the mind is under control.

Breath and mind functions are very closely related. As the breath is made tranquil; the mind can be kept under vigilance. Under this stage mind is always under control.

Increasing the awareness/consciousness can also help to manifest vigilance on mind. Awareness/consciousness of mind is Shiva constituent of the cosmos where as the mind it self is Shakti constituent— the power of the cosmos. By increasing awareness/consciousness of the mind, one is better channeling the flow of Shakti and reducing noisy and flickering nature of mind.

In short, if one really wants to control the mind, he has to be vigilant from all the multifold directions, but still the mind can jump at the earliest opportunity. Mind is just like a wind. Wind cannot be controlled, only if its energy is transformed, it will become less violent, so is the case with the mind.

In nutshell, all the above worldly horizontal positive efforts can make the mind less and less violent, but cannot control it fully.

In the process of breathing cycle, when breath is in, a human being is active with full energy, but when he exhausts/takes out the complete breath from the system, then for a microsecond in each cycle there is no breath in side, he is temporarily breathless during this interval. Then mind is spontaneously annihilated.

At this instant of temporarily breathless state i.e. in this discontinuity, he is with the Supernal unknowingly. In other words, scientifically, in this conscious-less period, he is beyond time & space; he has stepped in to be "Being". If this period is extended, he can contact the Supernal; and he can be longer in conscious-less state to be in "Being", and away from illusion/Maya.

It means at every breath cycle, a creature is with the Almighty in unconsciousness for a micro or nana second or so. A creature without breath is dead, so he dies once in each breath cycle and again revives as he takes the breath in, and thus a human being remains without mind for that short interval when breath is out of the body and fresh breath is not taken, since without breath energy human system is dead and functionless and so the mind. In fact, one annihilates the mind in each breath; and is beyond time & space.

Here lies the key, if a human being is able to increase this duration of being without a breath, he can put his mind more and more under control for a longer duration making it actively functionless, thoughtless, and in a state of complete rest for a number of times he breaths per minute. Less number of times in a minute if one breathes more will be his life span, and his mind will be much more in his control as compared to an ordinary being.

An ordinary man breathes approximately 21600 times in 24 hours. One can easily reduce this number by 40%-50%, and comparatively increase his life span. In other words, a void inside the system is created; Shunya, vacuumed inside by taking less number of breaths per minutes, and increased in duration being without breath keeps the mind under more and more control. This is the basic and easiest way to control the mind and to increase the life span.

Moreover, by the above process, a human being is more time in the state of "Being" and beyond time & space; thus, he is merged in conscious-less state away from illusion. In this state he accumulates divine energy with manifested self consciousness, which makes him healthy, wise and graceful, and he is able to extend his life.

Furthermore, to understand how the mind can be completely controlled, one must know root location of mind in the human body/system. As discussed above the human mind is Maya/ illusion, and Maya, being creator is everywhere in the body and around us. So, the mind is everywhere in the body and it is a part and parcel of Maya (omnipresent illusion). Since illusion is part of consciousness; so the mind is.

As it is so, the mind is diffused through out in every cell of the system and also everywhere around us like consciousness, in this world; in this universe; wherever, a human being wants to divert/ take it. In no time, with much more than a speed of light, it can reach/touch every part of the body, can go anywhere, and can also present in various locations simultaneously.

It is omnipresent like Maya, but its basic location/root is at the Brahamstanam—at the Ajna chakra – the point between the eyebrows. From here, it can go anywhere, in any part, so it looks it is present everywhere having being present nowhere. It is in consciousness, which is every where in universe but it is in beyond time & space in discontinuities.

Perfect control of the mind is achieved only by its mergence in the soul i.e. the Self, when consciousness is beyond time & space in a state of "Being". When it gets gradually merged, frequency of thoughts occurrence in the mind becomes less and less and wandering of the mind is diminished.

Thus, in the process when it merges completely, the breath becomes still and the mind instantaneously disappears; mind is annihilated. A perfect blissful and peaceful state pours in.

Furthermore, life force ascends from Muladhara to Ajna chakra; it carries by magnetic pull along with it the Jeevatma/personalised soul from the Dhahara/Anhata chakra through Visuddhi and

Lambika Chakra up to the Ajna chakra, located in between the eyebrows, which is the root location of mind. The human soul rests at this point and the mind gets merged in the soul gradually by concentration/awareness. Slowly all duality of the mind disappears; soul & mind turns into pure light.

The human soul & mind at this location passes from awakening to Dreamy state and then to Sushupati and gradually to Turiya/ transcendental state when the life force fully transformed to pure light. Gradually, this pure light travels upward to Chidakasha with slight awareness and goes through Unmani chakra to Sahasrara – thousand petal lotuses, before mergence with the Supernal. The mind completely disappears/dissolves at this stage.

Under such conditions, there is no breath, no mind, and no duality and thus the mind is transcended and the Sadhaka reaches to the perfect state of silence. This is the state of Savikalpa Samadhi. This may be Jagrik/Awakening Savikalpa or Turiya Savikalpa and may be Jagrik –Turiya and so on depending on state and percentage of mergence of mind with the soul. But, it is the state of silence, without active mind and breath.

Sadhaka/spiritual aspirant, thus enters into is Jada/achetan state without awareness and consciousness. A Sadhaka/aspirant can remain at this stage for about 3 minutes. This can only be achieved by the blessings of Almighty. After this, descending journey of light follows and gradually presence of awareness and presence of mind is felt as the light reaches at Ajna chakra. From Ajna chakra to Apex center, it is a pathless path of light.

But, now after descending the light after mergence, the mind gets separated from the soul gradually, but it has now changed permanently. Now the mind is no longer the original mind, bound in the Maya, as it was before the ascendance took place. The mind after mergence with soul becomes pure, perfectly calm without any prejudices, reactions and irritations.

After the ascendance, coming back to horizontal plane it has become from small to big, great and the greatest mind. Frequent mergence of mind with soul, soul's ascendance to Supernal and its descend from Apex center makes it easily controllable by the self, actively calm, concentrated and makes it more capable of taking complex and complex creative work of the world.

Human being can put his sincere efforts with devotion for this achievement, but finally success is in the hands of Almighty—the "Being". One must pray for mercy and Blessing of Almighty.

9

Breath Control–A Ladder for Personality Transformation

"Step into being"; to be beyond time and space with discontinuities brings virtuous inner transformation; it is to bring changes in the personality of a human being, which is otherwise really a very difficult task. Unless and until a person himself is not interested and fully determined to change his personality, it is not possible to bring any change in him.

Personality change purely depends on the self-efforts for a long duration along with complete determination and faith; this requires subjective in built mental resolution. However, if one follows the right path unknowingly for a long time, this it self will modulate his personality. Then the concern person will be himself surprised to know all that happened to him.

Scientifically speaking, causal, subtle and gross body of each one of us vibrates with certain specific frequency and with definite amplitude. There can be various frequencies in the spectrum of each body, but only a few and may be one or two may be predominant. Basically these frequencies govern the behavior pattern of an individual.

A person may be Satvik, Rajasik or Tamasic by nature; the specific nature of an individual is predominantly determined by the various significant frequencies of vibration by his gross, subtle, pranic and causal bodies. So, in short, unless the frequency of vibration in micro and nano-scale of causal, subtle and gross bodies are not modulated, an individual remains the same throughout his life so far his thought process, life style and pattern of living is concerned.

A dacoit can turn into a saint by the modulation of vibration pattern of his gross, subtle and pranic bodies. Indian history clearly brings out that dacoit Valmiki of ancient times, has changed himself to a saint of the highest order by reciting the name of the God "Rama" as "Mara" for number of years as he was not even capable of correctly pronouncing the name "Rama". This mantra—the name of the lord "Rama" has really affected the his gross, subtle and causal bodies——the Yantra of Valmiki i.e. his physical body to such an extent that gradually his Yantra, the body, started radiating Tantras—vibrations of the "Rama" itself.

This has modified the personality of Valmiki in totality and in due course he could write Valmiki Ramayana— one of the greatest epics of the world, which is worshipped and recited even today with highest respect by Hindus. This incidence is indeed the miracle so for change/transformation in personality is concerned by the recitation of the Mantra.

Similarly, Kalidasa, who was considered as the greatest fool through out his life, used to cut those branches of the tree where he himself used to sit, and used to fall after cutting these branches,. He could transform his personality by Mantra Siddhi and became the greatest writer, and was the author of world famous classic "Shakuntala".

In our time Mahatma Gandhi could change his erotic personality of his young age and could become "Mahatma" in the ripe age. He could liberate India by following the path of Truthfulness and Non-Violence in true sense by merely using his mental power. He could mobilize the masses by his selfless activities. His book "My Experiments with Truth" is a significant contribution after modulation of his personality with time, along with various other contributions including "Not by Bread Alone".

Now the basic question arises, how the transformation of personality takes place? By horizontal worldly means such as adopting self-control, imposing restraints of all kinds on the self, by different forceful means, one can temporarily effect/change his personality outwardly and can get some success, but within no time he will revert back to the original pattern of thinking, life style and habits.

Basically the kinetic energy of a person cannot be controlled by kinetic means. Kinetic energy can only be checked, but again the resistance inserted by the evil forces built in the personality in following this path will be so high by the force and impact of the kinetic energy of original old habits, thinking and deeds that forces an individual to revert back to the same personality as he was.

An erotic person by nature and with the inbuilt habitual inclination will never be satisfied by indulgence in sex with various women and by indefinite number of times throughout his life. A drunkard cannot satisfy him self by any other means except drinking although his liver gets affected.

Habits are the part of the built in personality, and these cannot be controlled by indulgence; and nor these can be controlled by non-indulgence by will power.

These habits can only be temporarily checked by horizontal worldly means and as soon as will power is loosened, the person falls back to his original habits. However, by deep awareness and watchfulness along with breath awareness, habits can be transformed.

Deep self awareness keeps vigilance like a proven non-local effect in science that changes the path of haphazard movement of particles in an organized systematical movement.

A hungry person can restrain from the food by the forceful coverage of fast on himself or by some other restraint, but as soon as that restraint is over, he may jump like a hungry lion or a dog on food. One can only control the self in totality when from inside or in the depth of his mind, he does not really in true sense wants or feels the craving for the same in-built original habits.

How a beggar can say that he has renounced the kingdom since he is not the king? .If a king says that he has renounced his kingdom, it has significance and honor, which indeed is the real renouncement.

In short, personality change is not the outward gimmicks and nor insincere temporary efforts. It is basically an inward change in totality; and it is really a very involved task that needs years of long craving for improvement and various practices for long duration.

By breath control, by Kumbika and by Shunyaka process, it is indeed possible to change the thinking process, and the pattern of subtle vibrations instantaneously to handle the situation at the particular moment. But, as soon as the effect of Shunyaka and breath control are ceased to influence, the person resumes the same personality. However, for years of practice if the pattern is really maintained, the personality change does occur.

If a person is able to change the rate of breath from 16 breaths to 8 or 10 breathes a minute in course of time; and if he starts breathing regularly and automatically 8 times a minutes in place of 16 times, which he was breathing earlier, then there is definitely a permanent change occurs in his personality i.e. from rajsik personality he could change his personality to satvik in nature. Then only he thinks differently, eats differently, and associates with different class of people.

The above clearly shows that his thoughts, words and deeds really got modified; since these are the subtle qualities, and have nothing to do with outward influence. The change of breath pattern has direct influence on human personality, and also on one's own longtivity.

To sum up it can be said that the easiest way to change one's personality is by full Sankalpa, and with complete determination as well as with the recitation of initiated Mantra, such that his body vibrates with the same frequency as that of Mantra and his body becomes the Tantra of the Mantra by divine virtues cultivated by the recitation of the Mantra. This is indeed a very long process, but without any shortcomings, risks and drawbacks. In one birth itself one can change his personality.

The accelerated way is to change personality is to go for breath control, change of breath pattern, and by Shunyaka method along with Mantra recitation such that one is totally immersed in the

Mantra during its recitation. This can only change the vibrations of the mind; and mind gets merged gradually in pure soul/consciousness under the effect of the recitation of the Mantra.

Thus, mind is annihilated, pure conscious transform into as divine light; then he enter in era of beyond time in timeless zone; from here he returns back with low energy and high frequency vibrations that transforms the mind, and in due course gradually his personality gets modulated.

Along with the above if human being follows the techniques of Prana control, awakened awareness and sky ness static vision, then the change of personality is accelerated since these techniques burn/remove the age-old impressions of Vasanas/tendencies on the human mind.

In short, self determination, Mantra recitation, breath control, Shunyaka, life force/ Prana control, mind awareness sky ness vision, mergence in timeless era beyond time/space, gradually transform a person with the changed personality; and make him a divine person who is adored by his achievement of divine grace in a very short span.

The above techniques are basically turning a corroded piece of iron into the gold just by the touch of Paras stone, which is nothing but stepping in timeless era for micro/nana seconds; this allows him to climb the highest peak of self-realization in this birth; and becomes Jeevan Mukta/ liberated soul, by modulating his personality in all respects.

By cultivating divine virtues, even if he cannot reach the highest peak, it must be remembered that any honest effort made by him in upward direction will positively raise him higher in all respects in this life, and time to come in the forthcoming life he will certainly be realized soul with the refined personality having all divine virtues.

In a nutshell, the easiest, safe and reliable way to personality transformation is to manifest the consciousness by being with the self; to step in to "Being" and to be beyond time & space with the infinite consciousness with discontinuities to manifest the self consciousness gradually.

However, the first and very significant step is to be with the breathing process; particularly with the discontinuity between the breath-in and breathe- out. This will enhance the subtle qualities required to transform the personality; in fact regulation of breathing is the ladder for personality transformation.

10

Breath Suspension–An Art to Achieve Silence

Silence of mind is very significant virtue that must be built in personality, and if not, it must be cultivated as an essential prerequisite to step into "Being" and to be beyond time & space. Silence is an integral state; and it is the most peaceful state of a human being. The silence state is basically wordless, thoughtless, and breathless state. On negation of breath and suspension of breath; mind is negated; it is annihilated; and silence appears.

In presence of breath, varieties of thoughts are sprouted and silence is withdrawn from the mental plane. Silence is not merely to be wordless; or just keeping quiet is not silence. To observe Mauna/keeping quiet is a primitive silence; it is outwardly silence. Absolute silence prevails when one is within the self and soul/ consciousness is merged in the Supernal; and one is in super-conscious state.

Other modes/types of silence are just the relative silence. One can easily communicate in relative silence when the receiver is also in silence. The higher level of relative silence can produce ideas, and it can receive the thoughts/signals.

In silence one can dream; dream state is also a type of silence state. Basically, mouth is shut but all the senses are in working state, and senses are opened to receive thoughts from conscious and sub-conscious mind. A mute picture goes on in the mind. It is a state of relative and a temporary silence state.

In short, in this dream state, one him self is observer but he is not awaken. If one is awaken then he cannot dream; he will be in dreamless state. Absolute silence is dreamless state.

The suspension of consciousness and sub-conscious states only lead to the higher state of silence. It is the state of mergence; it is the state of conscious-less with discontinuities. It is only possible when one enters from dreamy to Sushupati/deep slum state to Turiya/transcendent state when mind is annihilated, and breath is partially suspended.

In general, in the silence state all the sense organs i.e. Karma Indri as, Guyana Indri as and Tan mantras become functionless. Also, it is possible to achieve while using Shuniyaka technique, since under shuniyaka, there is no breath; as if the state of suspension of breath has occurred/ achieved.

Therefore, when all the Indri as/senses are function less then mind does not react because it does not get energy since breath is suspended. It has been established that mind traps energy from breathe; and so, under suspension of breath, the higher degree of relative silence prevails.

In this state, there is no provocation; and no objective-subjective, and nor subjective–objective reactions of the mind is present. There is not action – reaction in the mind; and nor any subjective or objective motivation operates in the mind. It is the state of higher degree of relative silence. However, as soon as any outside memory enters, the silence of mind is disturbed. Also, it can be disturbed even by inside sub consciousness thoughts.

Any mutative horizontal breath disturbs the equilibrium of silence. Breathe has multiple complex vibration pattern of external world; it disturbs the silence to the major extent by the multiplicity of thoughts. This may lead to propagate, and create the various desires that can ruin/disturb the inner developed silence partially/completely.

Basically absolute silence prevails only in the state of Samadhi/ mergence, and in the Turiya tita/transcendent states. In other states one gets only the semi-silence. By alertness, being in consciousness, one can prolong relative/semi silence by yoga practices. However, a simple breath can change the scenario of spiritual feeling, and irrelevant mundane feeling can pour in mind resulting in disturbing the silence achieved.

One must understand that silence is very mutative. No one can be in silence for a long duration by conscious and semi-conscious efforts. However, these are the only means to be in relative silence.

Ego in the consciousness can appear by Maya/illusion that brings various desires. Desires invite pleasures and memories, which give rise to grow other series of desires that subsequently attack the existing silence very violently. This leads to change the thoughts and affects the mind.

Above also, Provo Cates the mind leading to suffering both subjectively and objectively by spoiling the silence completely. On the contrary real relative silence achieved by consciousness and then enhanced by Turiya/transcendence state certainly brings absolute partial silence.

Absolute partial state of silence continues till the soul light/consciousness prevails and increases. However, if this state is transformed gradually into unconsciousness/unawareness state under the umbrella of soul light, it gives the bliss of absolute silence and happiness. Soul light is above any mutation and hence it gives real silence; it is the state less state of the Absolute.

Jeeva/living being is I- ness; and Jeeva, if accompanying the soul, it as termed as Jeevatma i.e. personalized soul. It affects the sanity of soul; its true divine light; and hence the absolute silence cannot prevail in the presence of Jeeva/living being. Therefore, desire-less attitude and rebellious attitude cannot be silenced and controlled in presence of Jeeva.

The silence can only be partially established if Indri as/senses are properly trained to have qualities like that of a soul, which is non-mutative; so that the desires of Jeeva are temporarily dissolved. In other words one must be JITENDRYA – the winner of the dynamic desires of the senses/Indri as so as to be in silence without getting provoked by any gimmick and desires of the senses.

One needs to propitiate the breath, so as to negate it by its own mercy to merge into the silence; such that breath does not disturb to be in silence. One must learn the art to be PAWANJAYA–winner of breathe; and he must be able to command the breath.

Existence of breathe in the body shall be in his control, so as to be in the zone of silence. The silence is the super commander; but it can be destroyed by any horizontal/worldly urge very easily.

Alertness/awareness/consciousness is to be strictly observed to prolong the silence state. There must not be any reaction because of any type of the horizontal worldly disturbances; one should be in ROCK LIKE SILENCE. It is only possible when aspirant is above the limitation of consciousness; he must be beyond consciousness.

Any type of consciousness in the horizontal plane including sub consciousness must not disturb the silence. All subjective and objective symptoms of any kind are to be nullified and must be shed down.

Shunyaka and breath suspension are the most effective techniques to invite and enhance the silence. However, any horizontal breath can disturb the silence any moment. The silence zone is very delicate and very critical zone. Prolonging/elongation of the silence in the human life are really very difficult tasks like Kukukshetra Sangarama/war. It is extremely difficult to increase the period of silence; it is just like to arrest the wind without solid boundaries.

Silence cannot be achieved by physical and mental efforts. If by active conscious efforts, the silence is tried, then there are chances that one suffers in sub conscious state; and many disturbances are surfaced again and again on the conscious level from the sub conscious state.

Any sub conscious feelings always try to disturb the silence with full vigor. So the memory of the sub conscious should be avoided by using Shuniyaka/void methods. However, it is very difficult to control the higher forces of microcosm and macrocosm, and avoid them to react so as to maintain the achieved silence.

One could only forcefully and consciously try such that sub conscious thoughts must not make the unknown linkages to disturb the silence. Even reacting and answering the conflicting issues might disturb the achieved silence.

The best approach is just to observe the thoughts; one must witness the thoughts without any reaction; any good or bad thought must be observed; witnessed but not entertained. Soon the thoughts will disappear and silence state will be continued. In short, thoughts must be taken as uninvited guests.

Some times one has to keep artificial outer behavior to avoid the conflicts, but inside poison of disturbances may churn more violently to create an era to destroy the inner silence. However, one must always try to get fake silence inwardly if the external conflicts are severe, and beyond control; but it will be far way from the real inner silence. This is needed practically in life since no situation under any condition is in our control.

To live in the society one has to become outwardly CIVIC by keeping/observing the fake inward and outward culture of silence. However, for a long time such action and reaction of the outward conflicts cannot be avoided easily. These are very mutative. By ocean of inbuilt inner silence and philosophical inward inclination, this can be made possible. To keep silence one must act subjectively, but objectively one must not react.

To be silent one needs to learn this art of being INACT. It basically requires separating the inner world from the outer world; this is the only judicial way to be inwardly silent. Tide and waves of disturbances of outer world must be kept on the surface, and inwardly one must be silent and calm like an ocean.

This above technique is the art of enactment to make the fortress of inward silence. INACTMENT is only feasible by having complete command on breath; by being consciously alert; and by controlling one's own emotions and reactions etc. The best approach is to observe the breath silently to divert the mental attention.

Enactment way of control to keep silence is not easily possible for one's own kith and kin. If one is disturbed inwardly in sub consciousness then his outward silence positively gets affected.

The only way is to shield sub consciousness by all possible means and conquer over rebellious thoughts of actions/reactions to preserve silence.

However, even for a highly spiritual advanced aspirant, it is not easily possible when one's own nearest are involved. To be with the breath silently is the only way; to be with the discontinuity of the breath is very effective; however, it is difficult to maintain and continue with time.

By controlling the self/own outward reactions, the inward silence is likely to be positively disturbed. But, for a common worldly man with his outward reactions, the sub consciousness is not affected since he lacks sensitivity being unrefined. But, spiritual aspirant at times affects his mental and physical health by keeping MUTE WORD LESSNESS AND OCIFEROUS SILENCE till he clears his sub consciousness by rebellion thoughts.

This above is because the spiritual science does not teach reactions and allows only actions, and at the same time makes a person highly sensitive. So in any active horizontal self-evolved problem/issue, an aspirant suffers to the greatest extent but for a common worldly man this is just a normal suffering.

This is because of suppressing of natural feeling of reactions to keep the outward silence by a spiritual aspirant. Its reaction to the inward personality is enormous and highly critical. Only breathe control come to rescue a sensitive person under these conditions.

In short, relative silence is mutative. To be in silence, the reaction of the self must be much less from an aspirant due to his capacity of tolerance. However, inwardly he gets disturbed because of the involvement in horizontal activities even if he follows the path of INACTMENT. Breath control is only solution for him.

The absolute silence can only be achieved in Samadhi/mergence; it is achieved to take step into "Being", and to be in beyond time & space. In all other states and controls, one gets mutative relative silence. This is only relative/semi-silence. For horizontal life even this is an asset to live in peace.

Furthermore, silence is Maya/illusion. Maya is arbitrary, mutative and so the silence is never permanent. It changes with time, space and causation. Maya/illusion is awareness/ consciousness, and so the relative silence is awareness. Being aware and fully vigilant one can save him self to fall down from the state of relative mental silence. However, absolute silence is the act of super consciousness; it can only be achieved to step into "Being", and to be beyond time & space.

In silence, mind is annihilated; breath is suspended; one becomes conscious-less with discontinuities; however, he returns to conscious state with manifested consciousness with divine energy.

This world is Maya/illusion so its negation is also Maya/illusion. Suppression of consciousness of reaction is Maya as well. It can sprout out of mind from time to time. Maya is Shakti/energy, and it can ascend vertically upwards. It is a Kriya Shakti and this is not different from source light. It is awareness/consciousness; and also a part of Brahma, the creator. Its dialectic possibility is Brahma.

Maya is very merciful; it is graceful; one must worship Maya then only it may give way for the transcendental journey to merge with the Supernal. By its grace only one can cross the barrier of relative silence/awareness to be in the absolute silence/non-awareness; it helps to come/arrive to the doorstep of Samadhi/ mergence.

It is basically to ascend from Para-Apara level to Para-Para level of silence i.e. from the conscious silence that is with efforts to the silence without awareness/consciousness and without efforts; it is possible only to take step into "Being", and to be beyond time & space.

If it is achieved then it is called Sahaj silence, which is nothing but the absolute silence. It is the stage of mergence of soul with the Supernal; breath is completely suspended; there is no breathing process in this state-less state.

The Para-Apara silence, being at the state of awareness, controls the memories of the sub conscious state that creates the sufferings in the relative silence. This silence has to work against memories and make the aspirant/Sadhaka to suffer much more than experiencing the actual happenings of miseries.

A memory of the sub conscious state is the worst. However, deep sleep is very helpful to forget such memories to ascend to the zone of silence. Sleep without dream is the best for the complete relaxation, and to be in silence without memories.

Silence is the rest of mind however conscious silence is illusion/Maya. Rest/peace of the mind is basically out of any action and reaction even if the mind is awake. Such state of mind is wakeful rest. Observations of fresh breathe to enter and used breath to escape is the wakeful rest of the mind. This is Maya/illusion.

Maya/illusion is wakeful and conscious activity with awareness; also, rest/peace of the mind even without action/reaction under these conditions is Maya/illusion i.e. the relative silence. Any moment it can be disturbed. Even a single ferocious breath can completely destroy the silence.

Maya-the relative silence cannot take the spiritual aspirant to the stage of Samadhi. Even in Turiya/transcendental state is partially illusion/Maya. And the divine light is Maha-Maya; it is much beyond the senses to conceive. Maha-Maya is mother and by her grace the divine path becomes approachable. It is Para- Para Shakti. It is Tripura Sundari. All of us beg for her blessings for success in the spiritual path.

One can only put his efforts, but granting grace is her prerogative and mercy. Maha-Maya is an active part of Almighty and only through this, silence can be achieved by following the vertical path and finally to reach un-manifested stage/Godly stage to be in absolute silence in the stage of Samadhi/mergence; to be beyond time & space.

One need not brood more on the past and try his best to forget past to come over sub conscious state; and then over come conscious state to finally land in the super conscious state of perfect silence. Tranquil breath is very helpful under these conditions.

If one does not learn to be silent in his life, he is bound to suffer particularly in old age when even kith and kin will not listen and follow him even his positive advice. Earlier one learns how to be silent, the better it is for positive and prospective living for him.

The other inner meaning of silence can be taken as detachment. If one does not feel concern, he remains silent; and in other words, it can be said that he is not attached; he is fully detached. By Mantra chanting, the inner silence can be enhanced. Silence is the power of God; one must be silent to be with the Almighty.

Generally, worldly people lose silence in views of the various problems being experienced by them from their kith and kin. However, it must be remembered/known that kith and kin have their own Prarabdha. We are just the instruments for their birth to bring them in this world.

Furthermore, silence is taught and understood by the subjective attitude; it is by physiological way of understanding the net situation. By objective means silence cannot be cultivated. Our soul, being un-manifested subjective dormant light is the institution of silence within us.

Our soul helps us in silencing the mind, which in turn is the source and guide to put full stop for the wondering of senses unduly for worldly issues/problems. Breath acts as a master to resolve the various complex issues related to mind and senses.

Consciousness is a very powerful instrument to maintain silence by self-efforts. Para silence in the hands of Turiya; Maha-Maya can grace silence both in vertical and horizontal journey of life. Sita, the life force meets Rama, in the Chida akasha through the Setu/bridge of Sushumna provided by Maya through conscious awareness of relative silence.

Hanuman the embodiment of silence did show humility even being capable of bringing SANJIVANI with in few hours; he did not act until Rama instructed him to bring for LAKSHAMANA when he was unconscious.

Silence is manifestation of capability and humility; and one must not misunderstand it even in worldly dealings. Even Ravana observed the power of silence during war with Rama, and instructed his own Vaidya/doctor to attend Lakshamana when he was unconscious. Ravana understood that this war is the Dharmayudha/religious war, so by the power of his mental silence and without irritation followed the ethics of the war.

This is all because of inner silence that guided him in the moments of crisis. Being internally in the state of absolute silence, he knew Rama-the Avatar of Vishnu-the God; and wanted to be killed by him in the war.

In short silence always gives positive results when one is not egoistic but silent. Agitated/disturbed breath can spoil the cultivated/developed silence. Yoga can evolve energy but cannot bring silence. Subtle ego developed out of Guyana/knowledge is much more dangerous than the gross ego, and can disrupt the silence within no time. Even great Rishis like Narada have failed because of the subtle ego, which lead him to confront with Narayana-the God.

In Maya/illusion, consciously one considers rope as snake; but when enlightenment approaches; ignorance disappears; even unconsciously one finds that rope is not a snake and vice versa. The best and the safest path to achieve silence is to be with the God; to be beyond time & space; surrender to Him; to come to SHARNA GATI to Him as a child; feel carefree and safest as a child with the mother. Mother takes full care in all respects and keeps the child comfortable. Surrender brings PARA MOUNA-the absolute silence.

Death is the mode of permanent silence; however suspension of breath is the path of silence. To be conscious of silence is the relative silence. SADA SHIVA; the mergence of Shiva and Shakti; soul and Supernal and the Samadhi are the absolute silence.

And it is easily possible if the life force penetrates Ichha Nadi/gate at Dhahara chakra, then it passes through APOORNA BHAV NADI that leads easily to Supernal; mergence; Samadhi; and state of absolute silence.

Thus, it is seen that various factors govern the silence; and all are in the hands of Almighty since ABODE OF SILENCE is the God himself; it is to take step into "Being" and to be beyond time & space.

In short, silence is the highest state to absorb the divine energy to manifest consciousness for healthy and happy extended life. However, breath is God; it enlightens by projecting different means and direction to be healthy, happy and to transcendent of time and space.

11

Tranquil Breath to Control Stresses

In present modern life a person revolves around the stresses only. There is stress in every walk of life. From the birth to death one moves in and out of the stress only. Nobody in this world is above the stress. Stress has become the part and parcel of modern life. Even each one of us breathes in stress irrespective of the age.

Stresses due to job, spouses, family, health, children education, their welfare, environment, social pattern, money matters, difference in thinking/opinion, surrounded by evil thinkers, deceivers, involvement in interactions and various other unforeseen causes create mental stress. This affects health and peaceful living even if one tries to be desire less, and tries to live in minimum worldly comforts without undue hurting others, and revolves to live with the self.

Number of stresses of day to day living in the materialistic world in a horizontal worldly plane can be tackled on being selfless, desire less without undue mingling with others; still many stresses that are getting generated by vulnerable social elements, which are beyond the control of the self, and just cannot be avoided.

A sincere, honest and divine person gets affected very severely and at times conditions become so miserable that he does not know what to do by his own knowledge of self-control and positive living. It is rather difficult to imagine a situation for an ordinary person who has not passed through such a trauma in his life. Furthermore, for hypersensitive person i.e. Sadhaka/spiritual aspirant, living as house holder, such a situation becomes much more difficult and severe.

Before going for more details of the stress phenomenon, literally and word meaning of the stress has been defined. In the word 'stress', 's' stands for sensitivity, 't' stands for transient, 'r' stands for response, 'e' stands for evolvement, 's' for stigma and last letter 's' stands for syndrome. It means stress is nothing but a "sensitivity of a person towards transient response evolving stigma for unavoidable syndrome". In short, it affects a sensitive person i.e. a spiritual aspirant more than an insensitive person.

A common human being under stressed conditions is affected with high blood pressure, high blood sugar level, heart palpitation, mind irritation, sleeplessness and various other physical problems. At certain stage, the situation becomes very pathetic. Medicines may help temporarily, but the human system cannot be cured unless the causes of the stress are withdrawn.

To overcome and remove the cause of the stress is beyond one's own control, and added to this, sufferings due to physical disorders get aggravated. Gradually situation becomes from bad to worse. Although one tries his level best to tackle the cause of the stress problem by one's full efforts and capacity, but to resolve the concerning stress level issues that are deeply rooted are difficult to handle.

These issues need immense patience, involvement, compassion and peace of mind besides in depth subject knowledge, assistance, positive advises and above all, the God's grace. Even if one of these basic requisites gets distorted during the process of tackling the stress concerning issues, the physical ailments get manifested and become vividly visible. Stress reduces the life span, and contributes immensely to our unhappiness.

Now issue arises, what is to be done? One needs to deeply ponder on this. Basically, it is essential that one must have a philosophical outlook of human life, on the problem and on any of such related issues. It is to be clearly understood that even by being good, honest, and totally positive in outlook, the various problems and issues can come up in the horizontal worldly plane in day-to-day life.

This clearly shows that to be even perfectly good in dealings, words, deeds and thoughts are not the only requisite to lead a trouble free life in this world.

Finally, it revolves around the "Prarabdha" of an individual in this life after doing his level best to achieve his goal to tackle stress concerning problems and success in the life. At time nothing could be done and one has to suffer without his involvement in undue activity. Under such conditions, one need not to blame himself and nor his associates and friends.

One must be clear that this is the outcome of his past accumulated karmas, and he has to under go the misery as the reactions. It must be clear that life is a continuation. It is continuum with discontinuities. Even after death one has to undergo the sufferings in his new birth as the net effect of his bad activities of the previous birth.

Any problem in life comes to evolve him; finally, it gets resolved after giving some misery. In general, any discontinuity in life evolves a person and makes him stronger; it gives a therapy effect. So, the only solution is to pray the "Being" for His Blessings to get stronger to face the miseries and the crisis.

Prayers under such adverse conditions give courage to the mind and tonic to the body. Prayer means to accept the miseries, and to express gratitude to Almighty saying that even worst could have happened. He had saved him. One must have such positive attitude in life.

During prayer from the depth of heart, mind is concentrated; it is one pointed; there is no flickering and roaming of mind; this makes the mind annihilated. Then only pure consciousness governs the system and as this period is prolonged in the mergence with prayer; consciousness is manifested.

Gradually this consciousness transforms into conscious-less state with discontinuity; this brings the timeless stage; then one enters in "Akaal"–the timeless zone and merges in "Being" with discontinuities; he is transformed into "Being", and he is then beyond time & space spontaneously; and thus, he gets immense divine power and energy to face the stresses, and stresses disappear by its own.

It is very important to avoid all types of mental and bodily stresses because of other associated problems, while under the effect of miseries. Physical signatures of the body must be very intensely monitored by close attention of the mind towards the body.

It must be very clearly known that under the effect of the stresses, the basic systems, which get effected, are the digestive system, breathing pattern and heart pulse rate.

Under the effect of stresses, digestive system becomes more acidic; more acids get secreted; and hence diet must be strictly controlled; all types of acidic food must be avoided. Food consumed to be such that it does not give acidic effect to keep the digestive system healthy.

Under such conditions, breathing pattern should be kept tranquil as far as possible. It should be kept calm without any irritation to keep the mind under control. Breath rate must be kept lower as much as possible to retain the calmness of the mind. One must be aware of breath as frequently as possible and try to be with discontinuity of breath to be in peace and draw more divine energy from the Cosmos.

Mental stresses and bodily stresses always try to disturb the breathing pattern. So, one must be always very vigilant of one's own breathing pattern, and try to make it tranquil as frequently as possible to retain the control of mind. Tranquility of the breath is nothing but the flow of air more or less equally from both the nostrils.

Furthermore, it must be remembered that the mind gets energy from the breath, as do the other systems of the body. So, it is natural that only adequate energy to be given to mind, and also the energy given to mind must be pure, satvik and without any irritation. Excess energy towards the brain is to be avoided. It is only possible when the breathing pattern is completely tranquil and breath rate is low.

To achieve the above state some people avoid food; fasting is observed to reduce the energy in the system. On the contrary, some people eat more to have excessive sleep. One must be vigilant to one's own system and act accordingly.

It must be noted that with less breath rate, which is overall good for mental peace, but with this excess of toxins gets accumulated in the system, and this leads to increase the stress levels in the system. So, to tackle this problem due attention must be paid that the time taken for breath out should be more than the time taken for breath in.

In other words, gradually it is better to make air vacuumed in the system by exhausting/removing more of air/breath from the system, and taking less of intake breath to run the vital system of the body.

Vacuumed state of the system is the state of nothing-ness; divine health giving energy is drawn by system in this spontaneous void created by depleting the accumulated breath in the system. If this is observed all the 24hrs a day during crisis then the stress levels in the system will not increase beyond the threshold level, and mind will tend to be self composed.

This will tend to control blood pressure, heart palpitation, acidity of the system, and sugar level in the body and so on.

Furthermore, increase of air vacuumed or Shunyaka in the system improves the digestive system. Besides this Udana Prana must be increased /maintained in the system. This will add further to avoid any excitement of the system, and enhance the spiritual energy of the system.

Also, during stressful stage if Udana Prana is passed through Sushumana Nadi more frequently, this will enhance the calmness of mind and give rest to the system. Although under stressful conditions to increase Udana prana and its passage through spinal cord becomes more and more difficult, but this is the only way to self control and maintain tranquility of mind.

On the other hand, indulgence in intoxication and use of tranquilizers to suppress the stress levels will tend to affect the mind adversely to take right decision, and also tends to make the mind sleepy more frequently. The best and easier way to increase the Udana prana is to listen very deeply the mantra being chanted mentally and/or vocally in each breath taken by the naval movement.

In conclusions, it is emphasized that to control the stress levels in the period of self crisis in life, the best way is to pray apart from the best self efforts to come out from the crisis of the horizontal worldly plane. The key process is to maintain vacuumed in the system; to maintain breath in suspended state as frequently as possible to be with the self besides using all possible ways and means to resolve the issues by efforts.

All issues of the horizontal worldly plane are time dependent; and no issue is permanent. However, our attachment to the issues increases the stress levels, which is natural since all of us are in human form and ought to get affected by the blow of Maya/ illusion.

There is no escape for any one of us; Maya has to be worshipped to gain its sympathy; and to get out of its blows and influences. Maya, itself is Brahma since is created by Him. Maya itself can dilute its effect not by our fighting with Maya, but only by surrendering to this Almighty force.

In a nutshell, one's sincere prayers from the depth of his heart in the perfect silence mode, in the state of mergence in "Being", to be beyond time & space, to manifest the consciousness can only assist him and save him from all issues of stress and miseries of his human life.

Thus, one can manifest divine energy to have protection in all respects. There is no other perfect, safe, reliable and absolute solution. However, tranquil breathing is best remedy to dilute the adverse effects of stresses on physical body and mind.

12

Enlightenment–Through Cessation of Breath

What is enlightenment? It is very rather difficult to comprehend even for an intellectual. It is beyond words and thoughts. Words cannot describe it and human mind cannot express it on the physical platform. What is enlightenment and what happens after achieving this, only an enlightened person can comprehend but still it is beyond his words, thoughts and speech.

Physically/mentally it cannot be expressed nor demonstrated. Here experienced, experience and experiencing become one without any duality so it is even beyond consciousness and hence expression.

However, what is the first step to reach its door and/or, what qualities are developed and needed to be developed to reach its doorstep; what is the scientific approach to be in enlightenment; it is very mysterious; it is purely a subjective approach; it has multiple means and ways; there is not definite laid down path; it is pathless path; however, all paths lead to same destination; the ultimate source is same.

To get enlightenment, one needs to cultivate divine qualities; to achieve these divine qualities are one's own self efforts and years of divine practices and, furthermore still this ultimate highest grace of the "Being" cannot be achieved without His ultimate grace and Blessings.

One can reach merely its doorstep by various scientifically evolved techniques, but opening of the door of the enlightenment is purely by His choice and grace; it is beyond human efforts.

There are no objective means involved for enlightenment; there are only subjective directions and approaches; and these may vary from one individual to another depending on his mental frame, thoughts and built in characteristics. That is why Buddha has made explicitly clear that one has to discover his own way to enlightenment based on his temperament, attitude and bent of mind.

However, every human being can cultivate basically various qualities those are governed by heart and mind i.e. emotional and mental qualities. In other words knowledge and devotion are the two basic prerequisite to follow this path.

Knowledge by mental development and intellectual in-depth understanding makes this process very comprehensive, easy to follow and practice scientifically by devotion to arrive at the highest peak of this door step of enlightenment.

However, there are many pitfalls on the way of evolution that can take an aspirant of this path to the original backward level again and again, but still by his efforts and persuasions he can stand by devotion and self efforts and reach to the door step.

However, unless heart and emotional qualities are not fully developed, devotion and faith do not touch the peak, till then the grace of the "Being" and His door of Blessings may not be opened. Until that stage, one will be deprived from the enlightenment.

The path of enlightenment, the supreme knowledge, is very straightforward on the one hand and extremely difficult on the other hand. It is like controlling the high-speed wind without putting obstacles on the path; but still draining the basic source energy of the wind.

It is the path of total integration. It means human mind should be fully refined, pure and one pointed. Duality of any kind needs to disappear in totality. It is the single track path without any division.

It is similar to an integrated seed that can only grow, and can form a big tree. It can only give flowers and ripe fruit with time provided the seed is of good quality, integrated, and for its growth adequate amount of fertilizer, water, sunlight and other necessities are available. With deficiency of any of the required needs, the seed cannot grow as plant, and nor it can develop into a full-fledged tree to give fruits to serve the humanity for decades.

In the same way, when there is no duality, the mind is fully concentrated and awakened; it can do wonders and can lead the self to the path of enlightenment. There is, as if, a death of mind when it is integrated i.e. it is fully concentrated/dissolved/disappeared without duality; it is annihilated; and thus available energies are evolved to reach to the state of enlightenment, if properly directed.

However, generally mind is always disintegrated and fragmented and does not posses the real strength like as in a seed, which is integrated and perfectly in one piece without even having a scratch. If the seed is fragmented and scratched, slightly broken, it cannot grow; even if it has all other amenities in plenty to grow. It will be destroyed with time without any growth.

Similarly, human body can exist/live only in one piece, but if one part of the body is fragmented, body cannot survive/live. On the contrary human mind cannot sustain an integral form; it lives in different fragments, always roams and thinks of too many things at one time. Its energy is always divided. If it becomes perfectly integrated, concentrated; it is then annihilated; then mind being part of Maya/illusion vanishes.

Furthermore, consciousness is manifested since mind being its derivative, is annihilated. And, then manifested conscious is transformed to conscious-less state with discontinuities; then consciousness steps into "Being" and transcends time & space; and thus self/Atman/Soul merges with the Self/Absolute, the Supernal.

This state is nothing, but the state of enlightenment. This leads subsequently to manifested consciousness of human being since soul is the core consciousness, which is enhanced with divine qualities on mergence with the Absolute/Supernal.

A human mind is the source of thoughts. It is the natural characteristics of the mind. At time there are number of thoughts in the mind, and some times one thought after another comes in mind. Mind has infinite energy since it is a part of Maya/Brahma; and it always works on one thought or the other; it is always dynamic.

The first step to achieve and climb to the doorstep of enlightenment is to bring the mind to the "thoughtless" state. Thought process needs to be stopped. It is only possible when breathing process is fully controlled. Since breath is the prerequisite for existence of mind and thoughts; breath is the food of mind.

Breath cessation gradually becomes the ladder for enlightenment along with many other prerequisites. Thus, no continue linkage of thought one after the other is continued in the mind.

One must observe the flow of thoughts in the mind. Gradually with time, flux of thoughts gets reduced and mind becomes one pointed without thoughts. It is the silent state of mind before it is annihilated.

The mind must be silent like water in the deep ocean. Silence of the mind is its static state when the mental energy is fully concentrated. It becomes reservoir of energy and brings peace to the mind like a rich person with wealth and power. Silence of mind shows its intrinsic strength. One can think deeply and will not be easily perturbed when mind is completely silent.

Silent mind is only governed by emotions. Mother loves her child when she is in full of emotions. Her mind is completely silent; it is merged in child's welfare and love. She cannot think anything else except mergence in love for her child. This silence gives her internal bliss.

In the same way when a person is in the state of mental silence, he is emotional, he cannot play tricks, and he crosses the crookedness of life; he is beyond worldly gimmicks. He becomes a man of love for other fellow beings.

Gradually, a human being becomes divine personality, as he is merged in silence more and more. He becomes more devotional with time. His mind and intellect are sublimated with time and divine light gets gradually manifested in him with time. Thus, a prerequisite for enlightenment is established.

Gradually, such person himself realizes serenity of mind, peace and change in attitude and temperament before others. The colleagues, near and dear of such a person recognize gradually all these changes in his personality.

Under these conditions his consciousness transform into conscious-less with discontinuities; he crosses the boundary of time; he steps into timeless state, and to be beyond time & space; he is then in 'Akaal', which is the abode of "Being"; thus he steps into "Being" and becomes enlighten.

Thus, his consciousness is merged with unity consciousness as if light is merged in light; void experienced in consciousness becomes one with cosmic void of unity consciousness. Every thing has become one instantaneously; there remains no difference between God and experiencing one.

Furthermore, when gradually person enters in the silence mode of mind, he speaks less, and eats to live and not live to eat. He gradually transcends his five senses. By proper living and with healthier attitude of life, his relationship with others and his own health improves.

In-addition, less speaking and use of controlled words by appropriate use of the tongue helps him to establish healthier relations with all, and this helps him to preserve his energies.

Silence of mind teaches him to speak with eyes and gesture of face, which will be true reflection of his heart. Child like innocence will be developed in due course with the purity of heart. He starts looking within and starts spending time with himself that enhances the scope of enlightenment gradually.

Thus, scope of booming the internal energies are enhanced, which helps him to remove vices from his mind and gradually mind will become pure and silent, and then he may experience the light of the self. The light of the self is basically self-enlightenment and the God's realization.

Furthermore, such a person becomes innocent internally in the real sense. An innocent person automatically becomes truthful, honest, fearless, and selfless; his egoism disappears and many divine qualities just pour in his personality.

Such a person will be near to the divinity as he will be away from many vices; he will be less and less in Maya/illusion, however, with discontinuities; so, he will be at least on the first step of enlightenment.

All the qualities, listed and analyzed, as above, will place him on the first step of the divine path. However, nothing is feasible without the control of breathing and the existence of tranquil breath. Gradually, manifestation of divine qualities by self-efforts, divine practices by devotion and His Blessings, and to transcend time & space frequently, are enhanced.

Thus, more and more divine qualities will be manifested; and thus gradually perfection in these qualities will finally positively lead him to the "Enlightenment" and "Self Realization".

In this way, he may achieve the highest goal of his life.

Thus with the booming divine energy, he improves his health; extends his happiness and well being; certainly this will add to extend his life. However, in the back ground is the science of secret of breath that guides him on every step to be enlightened.

13

Pranas and Evolution–Mystery of Breath

Life force/Prana Shakti are the mysterious part of breath. The air, we breathe, contains life force/Prana along with oxygen and other constituents. How this Prana exists in the atmosphere along with air, around us, is a spiritual, scientific and a mysterious mystery.

Atmosphere in which we breathe is a disinfected medium. It cleans all the toxins exhausted by the creatures instantaneously; and always remains disinfected under all normal conditions. There is no scientific explanation to explain this continuous natural process happening in the atmosphere; it is mysterious mystery of the nature; it may be termed as divine miracle.

Furthermore, one can live without food and drink for quite some time, but not without the breath and the life force; Pranic energy. Human being is dead without breath; breath give subtle energy to the human system; no breathe, no life; it is the dormant life force.

Moreover, breath is the only refined mode of transmission with the cosmos, universe; it is in built communicating medium with each other for all living beings in this world. It is the only practical linkage between inner and outer surroundings. Inner system is badly affected if the outer surroundings are not healthier and infected.

After the breath is taken inside through nostrils, it becomes Shavasa that which gives "Vasa" energy to Shava, "to dead"; it means breath energizes the body. Prana Shakti/life force is separated at the Visuddhi chakra at throat region from the Shavasa.

This Prana Shakti is further transformed in Vayana Prana at the heart region at Dhahara chakra. From where it gets distributed in the human system and keeps the system and vital organs working by the Pranic energy/life force. It has also been visualized that breath is transformed in Prana Shakti at Dhahra chakra too, located at the heart centre.

There are total ten types of Pranas in a human body. Out of which five are very significant. They have very specific role to play to make the human body healthy, and at the same time help the Sadhaka/aspirant for mergence with the "Being", the Supernal.

The important Pranas are: Prana, Vyana, Samana, Udana, Apana, Naga, Karma, Kurkara, Devdata and Dhanjaya. These are transformed from the breath energy in the human system.

The process of transformation of breath energy into life force/ Pranic energy has not yet been conceptualized neither spiritually and nor by science; however, existence of life force in the human system has been established by various modes. The Pranic energy of the breath is transformed into Samana Prana, the vital energy, at the Manipura and Swadhisthanam region.

The Vyana Prana distributes the Pranic energy of the Samana Prana. Depending on the needs of the different organs of human system, Samana Prana is distributed. Apana Prana in the lower organs is generated/converted from the vital Prana Shakti. Apana Prana helps for secretion, and the functioning of the excrete system; also, it removes waste of body.

These Pranas are self generated in the system by the Pranic energy of the breath, and is automatically distributed in the system by the auto regulatory process; however, their process of generation is great mystery.

Apart from the above four types of Pranas i.e. Samana, Vyana, Apana and Vital Prana/Prana shakti, as discussed, Udana Prana is required to be generated in the system by the close interaction/ impact of Vyana Prana, Vital Prana with the Samana as well as Apana Prana at the navel center.

By the mutual impact of these Pranas, one set of Pranas moving downwards and another set moving upwards, create a new Prana that is named as Udana Prana. This newly generated Prana by the impact of four Pranas is basically a life force and the spiritual energy.

The Udana Prana can also be generated by the recitation of the Mantra giving impact to the navel region, and listening the same deeply by concentration of the mind through the own ears. The movement/disturbance of the naval region by mantra recitation generates the Udana Prana.

Kriya yoga technique also generates the Udana Prana that increases the spiritual energy.

Furthermore, breathing through by movement of naval region, in and out, and by deeply mentally observing this process, also generate the Udana Prana/ spiritual energy. By the yoga Sadhana this Udana Prana is brought to Muladhara chakra, and from there it is allowed to ascend by yoga practices to higher centers; and gradually this passes through Swadhisthanam and Manipura charkas; and consequently, it reaches to the Dhahara chakra, the heart center.

At Dhahara chakra, it penetrates either on Rama Dwar/gate or Arama Dwar/gate or at the Ichha Dwar/gate. If it strikes at Rama gate, spiritual aspirant gets the feeling of happiness. It's penetrating at Arama gate gives the dual feeling of happiness and sadness because of the problems/miseries on the horizontal worldly plane.

If life force at Dhahara chakra strikes at Ichha Dwar/gate, aspirant feels the state of Apoor Bhava. It is the blissful state at Dhahara chakra. And if life force penetrates directly from naval centre correctly at the Ichha gate, it can ascend with high kinetic energy and easily reach to Apex center on passing through Visuddhi chakra, Lambika chakra and Ajna chakra.

At Dhahara life force gives Nada of Hreem and Aum automatically. If life force penetrates at Rama or Aroma gate, the chances for reaching the Apex centre is remote. This may happen because of the lack of transformation of magnetic functional energy from the Dhahara chakra into the life force at this gate, which may not be adequate to reach the highest center easily.

In general, Udana Prana increases the spiritual energy in Sadhaka/aspirant, and by its help when it crosses the Dhahara through Ichha gate/Nadi, it takes with it the Jeevatma i.e. personalized soul to the Ajna chakra after getting it purified at visuddhi and Lambika chakra. Sadhaka can himself understand easily from where the life force has penetrated.

Udana Prana/ life force is the carrier of the soul as the divine light towards Absolute. It is sky ness carrier of the spiritual energy. Each one of us has this energy but it is required to be generated, directed, felt, worshipped and finally to be taken along with the Kundalini power and soul to the abode of silence converting it into the light at the Ajna chakra, then via Unmani chakra to the Supernal/Absolute.

There are other sub Prana named as Naga, Karma, Kurkrara, Devdata (Vayu) and Dhananjeya. These are basically required to carry out the reflex functions of the body like eyes closing/opening, removing the Vayu/air from the digestive system by burp/Dakara etc., vomiting function when system needs to vomit etc.

Out of these sub Pranas Dhananjeya Prana is very significant. By this Prana, which is trapped in the abdomen region, the dead body of a person gets swelling and bolted up. It is the last Prana, which leaves the body after death.

Sometimes due to various unforeseen reasons, it is not able to leave the dead body. Then before pyres is lit or before cremation, when the body is put on the ground, the breath trapped in the abdomen is released by lower organs by the impact of handling the dead body, and thus Dhananjeya Prana leaves the dead body. It is generally the last Prana to release from the body after death.

However, due to various unknown reasons if this Prana is not released from the dead body, the dead man comes into consciousness if this Prana travel upwards in place of getting released from the lower organs.

Sometimes, if it is not released through lower organs, instead it ascend to lungs and heart, then the dead body gets the consciousness even on the burial ground; and even before the pyres are lit. These are rare cases, which have happened practically, however very rarely. Such cases have been reported, and duly documented. This is all by the miracles of Dhananjeya Prana.

Basically, Dhananjeya Prana is earth bound and Udana Prana is sky bound. Both are located in the Udana/navel center/stomach. Dhananjeya Prana may act after death where as Udana Prana is made to act in the living body to uplift spiritual aspirant/Sadhaka to enhance spirituality.

In general, all types of Pranas are generated from breath, but these are linked in complex pattern with breath. Even in a dead body Prana that has already mixed/combined with food, can get trapped in stomach of a dead body with the partially digested/ undigested food.

This trapped Prana in a dead body acts as Dhananjeya Prana after the death of a person and it is present even at burial grounds. This may act as a tool to revive the dead body. This shows food needs Prana for digestion and it has the capacity to hold the Prana even after the death.

After death the Prana may leave through eyes, nose, mouth or ears. It all depends where are the inclination of Vasanas in the mind at the time of death. If a person wants to smell a particular odor at the death bed, his Prana may leave through nose. If he wants to hear melody, etc, it may leave through ears.

Similarly, if he is very much desirous to see or eat some thing, his Prana may leave through eyes or through the mouth, respectively. But, if an advanced spiritual aspirant is able to bring his Prana up to the Ajna chakra then it is certain that his Prana may leave only through the Apex center, and from no where else.

For yogis, Prana leaves as transformed light through the Apex center, and merges with supernal light. Leaving of Prana depends on thoughts at the time of death. Some Prana is always trapped as Dhanjaya Prana in the abdomen, and leaves through lowest centers only. This may happen sometimes after the death or at the time of death.

Beside above there is a Shastra/holy book known as Chhaya Shastra. This explains that by the help of size of Chhaya (image formed when one stands under the sun), one can predict at least six months before when the person is likely to leave this world. For spiritually advanced self-realized yogis, there is no Chhaya since they are full of light, but appear in the physical forms like common human beings. Demy gods don't have Chhaya/shadow.

In short, type of Pranas, their importance, their functions has been duly recorded from which location Pranas leave the body; also, what are the conditions that prevail to allow the Pranas to leave from the particular sense organs.

The highest achievement for an aspirant/Sadhaka is when his Prana leaves from the Apex center, and he subconsciously knows when he is likely to leave the body.

All this is by the grace, life long spiritual engrossment of an aspirant and blessings of Almighty; and to take step into "Being" and to transcend time & space, which one cannot achieve even after his best efforts and Sadhana without the wish of the "Being". So, prayer and His Blessings are the prerequisite for this achievement.

Furthermore, if one is succeeded to have full control on his breath/Prana, then he may be able to retain his health till the end of his life and he may leave his body in full consciousness without any ailment. Basically breath is life; breath is God; and breath is a mean to transcend time and space.

14

Discontinuity in Breathing

Our breathing system is, we firstly exhaust the inside breath and then take fresh breath. So, there exists time gap when there is no breath in side. This is termed as discontinuity in breathing.

In between the two breaths i.e. out going and the fresh breath that is on threshold to enter the human system, one remains without breathe for a fraction of a second. The interval without breath is the span of death. In this discontinuity between the breaths i.e. in this interval one is in the state of unconsciousness, he is without breath.

In this interval when he is without breath, he is beyond time & space; he is in the zone of Akaal; in timeless zone; he is in the "Being", in the spirit/supernal unknowingly. If consciously one can understand and experience this mystery of the divine nature, one can unfold the secret of death.

Each one of us is in the blossom of death 21600 times per day i.e. the number of times one generally breaths. However, this duration is extremely small. But, if it is integrated considering that some one breathes approximately 10 times a minute, taking 6 seconds for each breath with a gap/interval of one second between the two consecutive breaths, then it is not difficult to assess that a person remains nearly 30 minutes without breath per day.

In other words he is without breath 15-20 hrs per month, about 8-10 days per annum; and in total life span of 80 years, about 800 days that is approximately 3% of the life span, he is without breath.

It means in 3% of life time he is with the death/spirit/Supernal in totality; he is in the zone of timeless; he is in "Being", beyond time & space; he is conscious-less and without breath. It is miraculous experience if one is conscious of this discontinuity i.e. interval between two consecutive breaths.

By meditation, being in Shunyaka and by consciously observing the breath one can extend this period even up to 10%-15%; he can experience death if he can be conscious in this period.

In this interval, one is generally unconscious; he is in discontinuity. However, if he is conscious of this discontinuity by self efforts, he can be with the Supernal by the grace of "Being". Thus, he can instantaneously be beyond time & space in between the time interval between two consecutive breaths provided he is conscious or aware of this interval.

Mind becomes silent if consciously this discontinuity of time interval between breaths is increased without any stress. It can even become the continuum experience to be with the Absolute; it is this discontinuity that makes a pathless path to be in unison with the"Being".

This helps to draw direct cosmic energy from the Absolute as and when it is needed by the system. Gradually system will be filled with divine light.

Subsequently, this improves health, well being, happiness and the life span. However, the spiritual aspirant may not have any desire to prolong the life since for him life is death and death is life; both are the same for him. He becomes Jeewan Mukta/ liberated soul by the grace of "Being" just by increasing the time interval between two consecutive breaths.

This is the basic mystery of mysteries, and secret of life and death and as well life beyond death. Thus, he can be with the source light of the Absolute.

To be with the source light and Supernal is Sandhya; it is discontinuity. The interval between transmigration of seasons is discontinuity. In a year, there are six to eight seasons; so, there are equal number of voids i.e. discontinuities. There is a void i.e. discontinuity when one season changes to another.

Sandhya/pooja is performed at the time of twilight i.e. when night is going to transform in to day light; and when day is going to step in to night. Noon time, when before noon is transformed to after noon, and transient midnight time transmigration time intervals are pooja times. They are also considered as the time of Sandhya; these all are termed as discontinuity intervals.

Pooja/worship carried out during this interval is very effective; one can meditate effortlessly in this interval; this interval is discontinuity; it is the rein of "Being".

In terms of yoga it is the time interval between two consecutive breaths, when used breath is on the way out and fresh breath is awaited to enter. This breathless state of microsecond is the natural Sandhya. It is natural discontinuity; and worship during this interval couples life and death. In this interval life and death are closely knitted.

This is the best time to transcend time & space; and to be with the Supernal/ Being. In this interval of discontinuity, consciousness is manifested. This is the most appropriate time for meditation.

An advanced spiritual aspirant can do Sandhya/ worship/ pooja with every breath; in this time of discontinuity he can be with the Absolute 21600 times a day. He can draw more and more energy in consecutive intervals of breaths from the Cosmos. Thus, Sandhya/ discontinuity become continuum with time.

In this discontinuity, firstly he is totally aware and awaken then gradually he may become without awareness with time; at this stage he steps into "Being" and to be beyond time & space; thus, the Sadhaka/aspirant experiences the blessings of Samadhi/ mergence being with the divine light enjoying the nectar of divinity.

So Sandhya/worship is not the ritual as being performed all around, but in fact, it is the yogic mergence with the Supernal by extending the interval between the consecutive breaths. This is the science and practice from Sri Vidya, which is the mother of all the religions. This brings a spiritual aspirant to the stage of enlightenment that is the source knowledge, and beyond this no knowledge exists. This is ultimate.

This gives light to the soul and oneness/disappearance to time, space and causation. One becomes silent and experiences absolute silence within him; he gets the full glimpses of death being alive; and he gets enlightenment.

In this above transcendental state, mind, intellect and consciousness disappear, and soul merges with the Absolute/cosmic consciousness. This is the fundamental science of microcosm; and others are only the applied sciences.

In nutshell, enlightenment brings the knowledge of fundamental science i.e.: knowledge and secret of death; permanent/absolute silence; super consciousness; elongation of life span; health; happiness; well being; migration to the better world after death; and so on.

However, enlightenment is through discontinuity and discontinuity is through breathing; hence breath is God

15

Anger Control Through Breathing

The anger is in general sudden burst of mental energy. On such moments the person does not know consciously what is he talking and why is he behaving in uncontrolled way. When the storm of this burst uncontrolled energy is drained out, mind gets calm, one feels relaxed and then invariably he feels bad inwardly; however, outwardly he may not admit his animal instinct and inhuman behavior.

On the other hand, when this mental energy is allowed to release consciously, although outwardly it looks the burst of energy identical to the first case, but it does not hurt the self. On the contrary, it gives the feeling of peace since it was the controlled and conscious anger on the other for his/her improvement without any interior motives. It is for the welfare of others with the controlled forceful release of energy. This type of anger is shown intentionally for some specific purpose for the benefit of the fellow being.

Only self controlled persons, those have full command on their senses and breath, and are inwardly completely silent, can act in this controlled way without involving and hurting them self. Their sole aim is the welfare of the fellow being.

However, anger of the first type where sudden burst of energy takes place, is the most common in the society; it is common among the family members, and it is spread worldwide. This need to be well understood, analyzed, and to find the means to control it, is very significant.

There are various causes of un-controlled anger but basically it can be classified in the two main causes. The first is psychological; and second is physiological. Physiological anger is linked with the physical condition of the body i.e. physical sickness, high blood pressure, heart issues and other physical ailments. Where as psychological anger is linked with mind, emotion and other subtle conditions.

The physiological cause is the prime cause of the burst of anger under various conditions that shows unpredictable behavior of the person. Physiological anger can be managed by controlling and overcoming the physical ailments, but psychological anger cannot be controlled without self-efforts and modulating the attitude of life.

However, regulated breathe and stomach breathing play a major role in controlling the anger. Tranquil breath is a miraculous approach to handle the anger.

The anger due to the psychological causes is basically linked with the un-fulfillments of the desires. When desires are not fulfilled, these may lead/develop anger or depression in the mind of a common man. These desires can be related to material, sexual, power or may be of any other nature. The unfulfilled desires lead/ generate sudden burst of mental energy in the form of anger on subordinates in the office, on younger, peers in the profession due to various reasons; it may be just or unjust. Sometimes this energy can burst on elders and superiors.

Egoism due to position, due to money power or because of administrative glamour can make a person inflammable on the smallest issues. Environment, surroundings and social interaction can ignite such people for an insignificant and irrelevant issue, although he does not have any control at all on such issues; these might be beyond his mental inceptions.

Increasing time gap between breath in and breath out i.e. discontinuity between breaths can control the mental irritation frequency and then subsequently it will be helpful to control the anger.

The question is what a person must do if he really wants to control his anger and has keen desire to overcome it. So that, his peace of mind, is not disturbed under any conditions. Anger must work under his command and not that he is governed by anger and subsequently repents after showing the anger.

If one critically looks within himself, he can easily analyze the cause of anger for each incidence, but as a human nature, he will try to justify and will try to find the faults with others without blaming him self. For a common balanced human being "judge your self and not the others" gives insight regarding the causes of anger.

Broadly speaking, the one who gets angry easily is having very fragile and weak mind. Such people with weak mind are incapable of taking slight jerk of pressure of stress in day-to-day life. Or in other words, the wisdom related capacity of their mind is inadequate, and has a limited human capability; however, they may be very intelligent, capable in worldly/materialistic activities.

It is similar to the case of a milk pot having a small capacity; but pot is more or less full of milk; any excess milk, if poured, will be spilled out. In other words managing bigger responsibilities with more administrative power with less capacity of mind is the same case as of small milk pot, and excess of milk in it.

As on heating, milk boils and spills out from such a pot with little heat, similarly bursting of energy takes place immediately from a weak-minded person under slightest stressful conditions. So the remedy boils down to the following measures to control the anger:

The first approach is to reduce the quantity of milk in the pot to avoid the spillage of milk by the excess heat to the pot, so that the boiled milk comes up to the pot top surface but does not spill out. Similarly, power/responsibility from such a person must be minimized so that he does not get more heat/warmth/egoism of power of any kind, and so that his anger because of power egoism remains within boundaries.

The second approach is to use bigger capacity of pot with the same quantity of milk in it such that even by excess heat, boiled milk remains below the level of the top surface of pot, and never spill out under any conditions. Practically, in other words, the concern weak minded person must increase his mental capacity;

and make his mind more strong, cool and silent simultaneously so as to take up the irritant situations without getting anger.

In other words, the anger can be controlled either having less desires, less money power, less power of position, less responsibilities rather less than one's own capacity so that he is always conscious of his mental thinking and mental turmoil.

Generally, a conscious mind is not irritated and even if he is irritated and gets angry, it will only be an artificial anger–a conscious anger. In any case such anger will not harm the self and will be used only for the benefit/improvement of the other fellow beings without selfish motives. The anger will not be under the influence to fulfill one's own desires. Frustration and anger will not appear irrespective of desires are fulfilled or not, if one is mentally conscious, aware, awaken and self-less.

Actions, if performed like inaction, just for the sake of actions for the service of the human being without any ulterior motives, cannot create anger, unhappiness and frustration of any kind.

Furthermore, to enhance the mental capacity, divine subtle qualities are needed. These can be cultivated by controlled breathing, observation of breath in and breath out process beside Shunyaka technique and creating of tranquil breath in the system.

In case a person takes higher responsibility, more than his natural mental capacity, his irritation and anger in day-to-day life are likely to increase. To overcome his irritations, and to control his anger, he needs to increase his mental capacity by meditation, prayers to Almighty, japas i.e. chanting, being with the self and by increasing his conscious levels in his awakening state.

Thus by his positive efforts and grace of God, gradually his mental energy will increase that will make him strong, and he will be able to handle the situations without getting burst, and to release his mental energy with anger; rather he will use his mental energy in creative work and restore his mind in silent regime. In general proper controlled breathing is the remedy to control anger since breath is God.

In any case to overcome anger, one needs to change his attitude towards life. One must work with discrimination and with the sense of non-attachment. One must not manure the position to fulfill his desires.

Also, he must have positive attitudes in the background of his mental thoughts that the Almighty has given him this particular level/position in society whether lower or higher, to serve Him in the form of fellow human beings attached to him with the best of his capacities.

It must be understood that all rewards, failure and success belong to the sacred power; nothing in reality belongs to him; he needs to discharge his duties with utmost responsibilities and care. With such lively attitude in mind; he will be far away from egoism of any kind; and under any circumstances anger will not dare to approach nearby. And thus, one can become the master of his anger. Even if temporary any anger comes, it will get subsided without hurting his consciousness.

Besides the above, the food consumed, effects and influences the mind of an individual person. Rajsik/ hot/spicy and Tamsik/ sour/processed/ left over type of food, physiologically effects body and irritates the system in different ways.

The evolvement of senses (eyes, ears, tongue, nose and skin) with various irritable activities also act as the food for the senses; this irritates the mind appreciably through different 'koshas"/ layers/sheaths of the body; and this acts as an indirect origin for anger and irritation.

In general, self-restrain i.e. control of senses from undue involvement in undesired activities do help to restrict the psychological origin of the anger. Furthermore, if required, it is not harmful to enjoy the senses to the maximum extend and then by self experience after discovering ultimate futility, the sense pleasure get discarded automatically it self and then no self restrain will be needed.

In general, anger is instantaneous like a spark in day-to-day life. If one is conscious, it is checked at that crucial instant, it diminishes immediately. But, in stressful paranoid cases, it may take very critical turn that is extremely fatal for the companion and other fellow beings.

Paranoid cases cannot be benefited psychologically; and even medical treatment may not give long lasting solutions. It is very delicate, dangerous and suicidal to live with such rare and extreme cases although apparently it looks such people are extremely good, well mannered, and courteous; however, slight disagreement and deviation from their mode of thinking can be inflammable in all respects.

Various aspects of stressful behavior up to some extent can be controlled by slow, steady and by good chewing habits for certain class of such sufferers, and can reduce the intensity of anger in a very limited way. Also, stomach breathing is very helpful to have close vigilance on anger.

Anger is more dangerous than sex and greediness; instantaneously anger can spoil all human relations psychologically without any logic. And nothing remains except the thoughtless ash of spoiled and strained relations after the spark. This is irreversible damage.

On the contrary, sex and greediness damage, shuttle and disorganize the relations, but such damage of relations is up to some extent is reversible or at least can be modulated.

In a nutshell, one has to be really careful in handing the self-anger and a stressful angry person. Anger cannot be controlled by anger as fire cannot be controlled /checked by fire. It can be controlled with patience, forgiveness and can be instantaneously checked at times by "surrender" only.

However, one looses own personality by living constantly with stressful paranoid character. One must try to avoid such personalities to live constantly with them to save him without damaging his own mind, well being and happiness of life, and increase stress level in self, which can turn/change him as an angry person in due course.

The only way, if one wants to control his own anger, he must turn himself towards divinity, become spiritual from the core of his heart, and prayerful. With the increase of divine nature, anger will diminish itself and get controlled automatically without self restrain.

The egoism of such a person by divine nature will get dissolved by itself and without egoism, anger cannot sustain. Furthermore, proper breathing and witnessing the breathing process by awareness can handle the anger.

In short, to turn the face from the materialistic worldly way of living to the divine way of living; to step into "Being"; and to be beyond time & space with discontinuity is only unchallenged solution to control the anger and to face the angry person. There is no other full proof remedy to deal with this chronic epidemic.

By these divine means consciousness is manifested that enhances the divine energy in the system; it increases divine qualities; subsequently patience increases; mental control is enhanced; metabolism slows down; thus being in conscious state, in general one does not get angry. Even if he is angry it will be mild and conscious anger.

Furthermore, if one is consciously alert and mentally decides that he will not show anger immediately but after few hours of getting anger or next day then he will never be able to show anger since anger is instantaneous burst of energy.

In nutshell, manifestation of consciousness and being with the breath are the best remedy to control the anger and to handle an angry person.

16

Linkage Between Breath and Happiness

For a common man happiness is a relative, and it is always with respect to others. It is comparative; it is mutative; it is time bound, age bound and Yuga/Kal as well as generation bound. Happiness is time, space and cause bound; and it is also governed by various defined and undefined parameters.

It is an abstract identity. It is desires bound; under the influence of Vasanas & in built tendencies, it revolves around the outward actions/gimmicks for a common worldly human being.

From the above, it is clear that happiness is always transient. It is never permanent. One cannot say that he will be always happy if he is happy at this moment. Happiness is earth bound, and hence it is always in motion.

Happiness changes with time and age. A child can be happy with a toy but to a young man a toy cannot give happiness. And what can make a young man happy, for old man happiness are miles always from that. Happiness is like a twinkling of a star. It is like a bubble that can burst in no time. But still all of us are made to look for happiness.

Our whole efforts are directed towards a point that might give us happiness, but that happiness vanishes like a bubble, and becomes a void instantaneously. Where it has gone, dissolved/ disappeared? Mind does not know; but a mutative mind again puts its efforts to search for transient happiness; and this game of hide and seek goes on as long as the breath remains.

One executes all his actions through efforts, indirectly through breath and till the breath is there and till it lasts. All actions depend on breath and when he achieves the desired results, he becomes breathless temporarily to be with the happiness of his success; thus, he enjoys the results/outcome of happiness. However, the breathless state is transient, he again starts breathing to live, and happiness becomes a mist in due course.

In other words, in this mundane world, one cannot be permanently happy; what so ever he achieves, gets, even if he conquers the world. His happiness is transient so far breath is there; and one cannot be breathless to live to be permanent happy. So, happiness is a mist, short lived, transitory, and temporary. Basically, happiness is time bound.

One can run behind the happiness; happiness goes on shifting its center; one can go on revolving around the happiness but cannot get it unless one gets dissolved in it; and one cannot permanently get dissolved till the breath exists. So permanence of happiness is a mysterious riddle that cannot be solved in this material world. One can go on accumulating every material thing/good of this world but he cannot accumulate happiness, which is transient and abstract.

It must be remembered that breath is God — "Being"; one cannot live without breath. Happiness is instantaneous breathless state; this state cannot be prolonged to exist; without breath and without "Being" there is no existence; so happiness is transient and it can be made permanent when one merges with the "Being".

Happiness broadly can be divided into three broad categories i.e. physical happiness, mental happiness and spiritual happiness. In other words it is gross, subtle and causal. The gross happiness is the happiness on the horizontal worldly plane. People look for different worldly goods and try to acquire them with full efforts to be happy. It may be house, gold, diamonds, cars and so on.

Even after getting all material goods and comforts, one feels vacuumed in side; still tries to get more of them, but he never gets satisfied with his desires for accumulation. This aspect may be extended to sex, power and other worldly comforts.

Temporary one gets contented but again after a lapse of small interval one feels deprived, his temptations increase and he looks to fulfill them to be happy again and again. However, this well of happiness on the physical plane is never filled until and unless mind is satisfied with the accumulation of modern comforts and their frequent changes.

In other words unless and until mind develops the intrinsic un-necessity of undue accumulation of physical material items beyond certain limit, the mind cannot develop authority of detachment from the material goods.

If the mind accumulates wisdom with age or with existing knowledge that the greatest personalities of the world have left as posterity; it can assist a person for his physical, mental and spiritual satisfaction.

One must know that mind controls the senses. If a mind is made stronger from a lower to higher level, only then some direction of hope can be given to enhance the happiness. At one stage when mind turns into the greatest mind, he can command all the five senses i.e. eyes, ears, nose, tongue and skin that look after him to fulfill his desires and get happiness out of them.

In a nutshell, the greatest mind only can help/assist to make a person to be happy, by giving him positive direction. When intellect of a person accumulates gradually this wisdom, then happiness does not remain a mystery and person feels happy what so ever he has. It does not mean that he becomes idle; still he works much more efficiently but his actions are action less and they are selfless to fulfill the commands of "Being"; they are not for his selfish gains since his even essential desires become negligible or just are very limited.

In a simple mathematical language happiness can be defined as the number of desires fulfilled by total number of desires. So, if the total number of desires is less, the man is happy or if his most of the desires are fulfilled without increase of the desires any more, he is happy. But, if desires are increasing and not getting fulfilled, his unhappiness and miseries will go on increasing. He becomes miserable with time.

So in short, the happy man is he, whose total number of desires tends to be zero; it means denominator in the mathematical equation of desires is zero, and then only his happiness is infinite. If so, then only he becomes a blessed soul.

In simple words, it can be said that the Vairagaya or detachment of a person can only make him intrinsically happy.

Under such conditions, his breath will be calm, tranquil, and rate of breath will be less; he will be nearly in breathless state; this makes him happy and blessed; he will be in close proximity of divinity; he becomes divine in nature with time.

In general, physical happiness comes with the accumulation of material goods. Mental happiness comes with knowledge, and intellectual happiness one gets with wisdom. Each of this happiness can supersede another. Intellectual happiness can supersede mental and mental happiness can supersede physical; and thus higher happiness can control the lower level of happiness.

Basically happiness is what one is looking for. If one is looking for wisdom, wealth cannot make him happy; as Gautama Buddha was not happy with worldly pleasures and wealth. He wanted enlightenment so he could renounce all the worldly comforts.

Happiness is that which one is intending or looking for, other gains have no meaning for him. The happiness, one is looking/intending for, can generate tranquil breath automatically in him after he achieves that happiness. Basically breathing state gives happiness and this cannot be achieved without inner evolution.

All these types of happiness i.e. intellectual, mental and physical are very mutative; and one can never be satisfied even if having maximum of all of them. One can be really happy when his happiness approaches a blessed state of Sat, Chit, Ananda. Unless happiness is converted/ transformed into this state of Ananda/Bliss state, he will be lingering in the horizontal worldly plane to seek some happiness or the other.

Blessed state is only achieved happiness by the control of Prana Shakti. This is possible only by being breathless i.e. by controlling the breath and ascending the life force within him; and by converting this life force into the divine light. It means Maha Shunya state of the physical system or void/breathless state can only bring blessed state when happiness is totally transformed into bliss. In this stage no desire is left.

A desire less man is near to God. Man minus desire is God. It is only possible by breath control; it is the state of single Shunya; if it is coupled with Prana control—then it is the state of second Shunya; if it is accompanied with sight gazing/Drishti Tratak on divine light—it becomes the state of third Shunya.

By achieving the state of these three Shunyas i.e. in Maha Shunya/nothing-ness state, one can be in contact with cosmos; he can be with cosmic energy; and then only he is with the blessings of Cosmic Mother; thus, he is in complete blessed state and much more happier than merely with the physical, mental, and intellectual happiness.

Furthermore, absolute happiness lies in mergence of the Self with the Supernal. All other grade of happiness is only relative and transient. And this is possible/achievable with the Blessings of "Being"; however, sincere efforts to achieve the grace of Almighty do play a significant role.

To be conscious; manifestation of consciousness; to step into "Being"; to be beyond time & space, to be merged in to supernal; thus to be in conscious-less state with discontinuities; being super conscious; all this brings blessed state with manifested consciousness even when one is back to conscious state after getting merged in Supernal.

This is the ultimate happiness. Being in this state one is Jeevan Mukta/liberated soul. If one can get this state by Sahaj process than he is Mahayogi – the blessed soul and the happiest individual in the world just having 'no thing' but possessing every thing.

It is the state of permanent happiness; one can jump into this state as and when he wants if he becomes Jeewan Mukta. Being temporary–it is a permanent state since it is Sahaja/easily achievable for an advanced personality/liberated soul.

In short, it can be concluded that happiness is transient and can be made permanent if transformed into the divine blessed state being in the divine universe beyond time & space; and by the grace of "Being". It is possible in a state of suspension of breath; however, this cannot be prolonged in the state of physical existence; so happiness will be transient in the physical state.

However, in this way if one's awakening consciousness is manifested; his health, happiness, wisdom, well-being and life longevity is enhanced by the accumulation of divine energy in his system.

Thus, happiness becomes a stateless state of an individual even if on having every thing he posses nothing – but His/ "Being" grace, which is all in all.

The easiest way to be happy is to surrender to Almighty in all respects; one must perceive that God is the doer and he is just non-doer identity; all success and failure is His; he is not involved. So, there is no question of his happiness or unhappiness. One must experience this state of mind; this world shall be taken as His Drama; he must consider him as an actor of this huge universal drama, then he will always be happy.

As his way of perceiving is modulated, he will transcendent all happiness and unhappiness of this world; he will be liberated from all miseries. This is the key. To achieve this one has to enter the abode of silence in this life; he has to pass through the bridge of breath so as to be with Almighty force.

In fact, breath control; mindfulness of breath; being with discontinuity of breath are the key to be happy in this mundane world.

17

Pranayama–The Art of Well-Being Through Controlled Breathing

In this short span of human life, if a person wants to understand the Self, to be with the Self, to be a Self-realized, to merge in the supreme Almighty's consciousness, to be with the Almighty, to be in to the "Being", he needs to understand the Pranayama very deeply.

By the art of Pranayama at its deepest level, one can achieve the highest purpose of life–the Self-realization; through the consciousness, by the consciousness and in the consciousness.

As the name indicates Pranayama is the worship of the prana i.e. nayama to prana, which is living/life force in a human being, and it is generated by breath in the human system.

By the control of prana, the life force, by the art of practicing Pranayama and by the grace of God, one can merge in the Almighty/ Self; he can be beyond time & space. By the merger of an individual self/consciousness into the Almighty Self/ universal consciousness is similar to the merger of the waves into the ocean; it is like merger of wave water into the ocean water; finally only water remains without waves.

Under such conditions, self becomes the Almighty Self. Every thing appears from the Self/Being like waves and merges into the Self/Being. The disappearance of the waves in the ocean is the witness to the ocean /real Self by the waves; it is similar to the disappearance of the breath existing in a human being, which is the conscious witness of the Almighty Self in the human body cave.

It is the basic requirement that a person must be physically healthy to step in to for putting the efforts to be self-realized. An unhealthy person will revolve around his health only; his attentions will be on the unhealthy organ and on the disease, he is suffering from. He is unable to concentrate on any other activity unless cautiously he forgets all his physical and other miseries, and treat them as a part of their life.

In general, to be physically healthy, the technique of "Pranayama" is widely practiced. Various techniques of Pranayama have been taught in the Indian school of Yoga so that body gets more oxygen that burns the body toxins so that body becomes healthy and aspirant/practicer/Sadhaka may feel inner happiness.

Various techniques of Pranayama, by redistribution of air/prana breathed in, and conscious control of breath at different locations in chest, stomach, lower organs etc. corrects their functioning; this is done by the input of more pranic energy and taking away the toxins from the various organs of the body forcefully in shorter interval.

Pranayama along with appropriate food intake and correct life style are the basic requisites for the healthy living. Merely practicing of Pranayama does not render any apparent benefit without proper life style. Pranayama rejuvenates the body physically and increases mental capacity besides giving awareness of understanding of the purpose of life.

The deeper purpose of Pranayama is to be with the Self—the unseen power of Almighty, which is within our physical shell to prolong our physical life and improve our health.

It is easy and fundamental to understand that by simple techniques of Pranayama, breath rate of an individual reduces which increases his life span since each one is born with the specified number of breaths. This means our system is designed with certain fatigue life before it diminishes and become unhealthy.

So, it is natural that by lowering the rate of breathing increases the net life span automatically as per basic fundamental principles of mechanical sciences. Various modes and techniques are well established in the literature.

In the usual technique of Pranayama, holding of breath is the essential prerequisite. But holding of breath in any organ beyond certain limited duration is extremely harmful for the entire system. It is particularly harmful for people suffering from the blood pressure and heart problems. Unknowingly under ignorance, it has been practiced by number of individuals who have severely suffered in a long run.

Basically Pranayama is not the technique of unduly breath control to come to the stage of breathlessness just by holding the breath. And, thus, this is not to supply more oxygen to the system to get higher mental concentration by deteriorating the fine control of precise nervous system of the body.

Each one of us has witness in the life span that breath is automatically get controlled under critical circumstances, and then the person gets sunburn deeper concentration to act appropriately. If this is practiced frequently as an exercise for breath control for higher concentration, this may lead to very complicated health hazards.

Unduly breath control under the pretext of yoga to arrive at the breathless stage under any circumstances is totally unhealthy and very harmful. It should not be practiced by any norm. Yoga needs to be practiced under strict supervision for physical and mental health.

Automatic breath control happens during deep studies or engrossment, but deeper concentration to practice for self-control needs to be done precisely with deeper understanding to get the tangible results for physical and mental well-being.

Breathing process is an automatic natural process for survival. To mingle with the preset breathing process, one needs to have very deep physiological and psychological understanding of breath, which is the art of self evolution. Even research of modern science is quite far away from this aspect to understand except that of some knowledge of the breathing process and after effects of breath being controlled.

Breath control is the path of enlightenment; and physical science still needs to probe breath control process in depth; this is required to arrive at the deep root understanding to practice the art of breathing so as to approach to the gate way of the Self.

Breath is the only physical linkage between the external world and the internal system of a human being. Through breath one communicates with another. A living being cannot live without breath for more than a few seconds; although one can survive without water for a few days and without food much longer even for a month or so.

Air is considered as the master, and breathing is the process to have a ceaseless contact with the master /Being/God/Almighty. Physical survival of a human being is by breath only.

As soon as breath leaves the physical body and do not enter, a man is considered as dead. Although all the organs of the body including ears, eyes, all organs of action are intact immediately after the last breath leaves the body.

Our system works on an automatic intake and exhaust of the breath. Intake, exhaust and again intake of the breath are an automatic natural breathing process. However, between, exhaust and intake of a fresh breath, for a fraction of a second when fresh breath does not enter, a living being is in a breathless state. It is the stage as if there is no breath.

Thus, condition of a living being for this fraction of a second is like that of a dead body, when last breath is out from the system and fresh breath has not entered. This is the state similar to the dead person who does not breathe. In fact a man without breathe is considered/declared as a dead person. However, after a fraction of a second, intake of a fresh breath takes place automatically, and thus, in the human system, a cycle of life and death goes on till the intake and exit process of the breath is continued.

In other words in each cycle of breath, an individual passes through the cycle of life and death continuously unconsciously without any interruption approximately 15- 20 times a minute depending on intake and exhaust of the breath. The above process shows that life and death cycle goes on, and each one of us experience death approximately in every 3-4 seconds, but no body realizes this.

However, if some one some how by various spiritual practices able to extend the time gap between exhaust and intake of breath, he can cautiously understand this phenomenon world; and gradually knowledge and wisdom of the unknown mysterious sources can be perceived by the wish of Almighty.

The duration, when one is breathless i.e. the interval/gap between two consequent breaths, one traps the mysterious divine energy from the Cosmos. Since in this nano interval one is beyond time and space in conscious-less state; he is with the 'Being", so energy is drawn from Cosmos in this discontinuity.

This divine subtle energy simultaneously start getting accumulated through the concealed unknown means in our intellect, mind and physical system that changes our thinking pattern, and the way of living, and make us more creative in all walks of life besides giving us better health and happiness. Although, the effect of good and bad Karmas still one has to face as per the norms of the actions-reactions.

In a nutshell by reducing the number of breaths, and not by holding the breath, but by increasing the time gap between exhaust and intake of the breaths, and by various yogic practices one purifies his body. The gap between the consequent breaths can be extended by consciously observing the breaths without interfering their in and out.

Also, by taking pure satvik food intake without much of oxidizing products, by natural living; pure thoughts; without much of worldly excitements; divine thinking; by witnessing/observing the senses appropriately and friendly manners; one can reduce the stress levels of physical, mental and physiological system that can modulate the breath cycles and make the breathing pattern tranquil.

Subsequently, this will turn the system more relaxed that can increase the life span apart from giving the opportunity and glimpses that leads to integration of the mind, intellect and finally one can be nearer to the Self.

The above in turn will make us experience the state of the cease of the breath as if all the waves have merged in to the sea water;

and mental sea has become totally calm without any turmoil of the waves for the time being before the fresh waves appear. It is the stage of perfection, and door to Self-realization in the human life.

The automatic cease of the breath by the Pranayama techniques, and not merely by breath control makes the body to conserve its energy; and this fine energy if canalized properly can lead to disclose the new and fresh dimensions of the mysterious world that help us to be nearer to the Self light and be Self-realized in due course by the grace of Almighty's mysterious force, the God / Self.

Furthermore, it takes us beyond time & space where our consciousness joins the Cosmic Infinite Consciousness through no-local effect; thus our conscious is manifested. This enriches us with divine qualities besides making us healthier and extending our life. This is the miracle of breath.

In short, Pranayama is a breath modulation technique, which gives us health, happiness, well-being and transcendence of time and space to be with infinite Cosmic power–the Almighty.

18

Experiencing Death Within Life Through Breathing

To understand the concept of death is very mysterious and complex. Moreover, it is more difficult to understand death within the span of life. If one can experience death in his life then he will not have any fear of death. Then only he can live in death as he lives in life. For him death and life both become the same.

Experiencing death in life is the death of Maya - the illusion. He can raise himself above the Maya if he feels/realizes/experiences death in life. Then only mystery of life and death will be clear to him while living.

Feeling/realizing/experiencing death is nothing but the end of the cause of the cycles of his ego and Sankalpa. It means all his ego and Sankalpa will disappear and he will start living just for the sake of living as if he is mentally dead but physically alive.

His experience of life and death become simultaneous. He lives without any desires, and so leaving the physical body/form is just a play for him since he lives without any attachment of any kind with any one.

Basically, he is very close to death being alive. Neither gimmicks of life attracts him and nor death creates any fear in his mind. For him there is no duality of life and death, he is very friendly and close to both. He loves death as he loves life. Death for him is just coming out from the closed room to the open sky.

Such a person is the realized soul and he is the man of real knowledge and wisdom. He has full control on his breath. He forgets and lives in transient death 21687 times per day, the number of times he breathes. By suspending his breath, he can be with death /spirit. He has full command to be with life or to be with death as per his wish.

Desires come from the depth of the heart from Jeevatma/ personalized soul; and these are instruments to force an individual to live to fulfill them through planning by mind and execution by ego. Food is the cause of extension of life, and cause of the breath to digest the food. Food gives energy to live but it is illusion to think that one lives by food only. One can live on water and gradually can switch on living entirely by the energy of the breath.

Air, we breathe, has all the elements that can keep our body fit and healthy, since through air our physical system extracts Pranic energy that gives basic support to live. Jeeva needs more number of breaths to digest the solid food; and thus it is more under the influence of Maya/illusion. By minimizing quantity of solid food, one can gradually conquer Maya and can live more with the spirit, and gets closely associated with the death.

Food creates more desires; increases ego; and layers of Maya/ illusions go on increasing on the Jeevatma. After fulfillment of one desire, another desire is poured in, and thus unending cycle of desires is continued. Thus Samhar Biza, the extension of desires continued without any restrain that increases the love/desire to live, but fear of death always scares an individual. However, when the desires are diminished, one can be in a state of silence. Indeed death is a state of absolute silence.

By death of all the desires and suspension of breaths as well as manifestation of consciousness/awareness, one can get the glimpses of enlightenment by the grace of Almighty; and he can become immortal. Away from the food and breath; and being in manifested consciousness lead an aspirant/ Sadhaka to the doorsteps of death being in this life.

The optimum way is that one must eat to live but not live to eat if he wants to perceive mystery of death in life. Becoming pure

Satvik, living on just water and finally on air/Prana, increases the soul light that helps to merge the soul in to the Supernal, and this gives glimpses of experience of death in life much faster.

Mergence of soul with Supernal with discontinuities; transcendence of time & space; discloses the mystery of death in life, and life beyond death. This is possible by having full command on breath.

Only Jeeva/living being passes through the agony of death. Soul is supreme and it is beyond life and death. Realizing the soul light being in this life removes the curtain of death, and one becomes liberated from the pains of life and death forever. He becomes the enlightened soul and this is the highest aim of one's life.

In short, death within life is: suspension of breath; manifestation of consciousness after being conscious-less; to be desire-less; transcendence of time & space with discontinuities; and to be self realized. Without the mercy of breath, this mystery cannot be perceived; that is why breath is God.

To perceive death within life is the art of transcendence of breath while alive as and when some one wants to experience death within life.

19

Visualizing Mystery of Life and Death Through Breath

Every one of us is surprised to know that life and death exist simultaneously in the process of existence in our life. In every breath each one of us is born and dies. This process goes on life long. In the breathing cycle, as the fresh breath goes in, one gets life with vitality and as the breath goes out, he dies instantaneously till the next fresh breath is resumed. If the next fresh breath does not come, life of the living being is under stake.

The time spent without breath till the fresh breath is not in i.e. the time spent in the void, indicates the death of the living being in such moments. So, life and death exist simultaneously in the span of life in this world in each breath cycle.

It is surprising to know that in our spinal cord, two serpents are closely intermingled to each other. One of them is visible snake that is the divine light in the life; and other one is invisible, which is the black snake of death. Both these serpents are coiled together and projected with separate hoods. Both are anti-poles to each other; one is life giver and other one is the life taker. Both are complimentary to each other; and have distinct functions. Human survival depends on both of them; survival is at stake, and not feasible if one of them is functionless.

Snake of death, the black snake, consumes the toxins of the body and keeps it healthy. It helps to excrete toxins by Apana Prana, Apana Vayu and helps the Udana Prana to function. Snake of divine light moves the human life. Thus, both life and death forces i.e. white and black snakes are in unison and are in love with each another.

The love of these snakes is through breath. One takes the fresh breath; other exhausts the used breath; and thus the continuity of breath in and out is suitably maintained. If the used breath is not out of the system, the fresh breath cannot enter. So, it is evident that fresh life can only come when process of death is actively continued.

It must be remembered that death only brings fresh life, and so if there is no death, then there is no life. Life and death are continuum, neither death can exist without life and nor life can exist without death. Life is manifested Brahma/God, and death is un-manifested Brahma/God. Both are the separate poles of the same existence.

Birth of any living being ends up with death; it is the law of the nature; so one must not be scared of death. When each one of us dies with every breath; then life beyond death, and life prior to death are no more mystery. It is continuous unending process and parts of existence in different states. These are well experienced by the Self-realized souls.

Both white and black snakes i.e. Kundalini/divine force and death exist in Kula Chakra. In the wakeful and dream states, their existence is felt. In Sushupati state, both are in the state of Rati i.e. they are in unison. In Turiya, firstly the blackness/darkness, the indication of the presence of black snake, is visible; prior to the soul light i.e. the presence of kundalini, the white snake appears.

Turiya/transcendence of time & space is the state of temporary death; the state of lack of function, where the light of Kundalini is firstly consumed by the black snake of death. After consuming positive divine energy of light, this black snake gets engaged in its own assigned activities of withdrawing toxins of the physical system, and then only Kundalini, the serpent of divine light ascends and merges the soul with the Supernal.

The state of Sushupati is the root/location of the union of death and life where death acts as a role of the husband, and life acts as a role of wife. Wife as a sign of divinity and glamour; she acts as a divine power, and is brought up for the Godly activities. However, the husband, the black snake, the death engages him self for the mundane worldly activities of preserving, maintaining, cleaning and conserving the human body/form.

Out of love, husband, the serpent of death takes care of life, his wife, the divine Kundalini power, and helps her to boom up. Otherwise life, the wife, cannot be glamorous and boom up; if death, the husband does not co-operate. This is the real mystery of life and death in the span of life and spiritual evolution of a Sadhaka/spiritual aspirant.

Furthermore, food is essential for living; it is properly digested by the interaction of various Pranas; and finally the intestines absorb Anna-Rasa i.e. secretion of food, and thus life moves.

Black snake take energy from Anna-Rasa for survival just by touching/kissing the white divine snake; it executes body functions to keep the body fit in all respects by removing excrete and other dead stuff of the body by creating Apana Vayu; and thus making/cleaning the path for the Kundalini to ascend to fulfill its final goal.

The same food can kill the white snake when breath seizes, and Pranas become functionless and food remained undigested, then it gets converted into poison in the body. So, breath is termed as life; it is the manifested God.

The same food, which is the source of energy for both the snakes, finally turns into the cause of their death. So Anna-Rasa, when consumed by these snakes creates hunger, it gives life; and when food is undigested, it causes death as if it swallows the serpent of life.

As the serpents lay eggs, eat part of their eggs and hatch part of them that become snakes. In the same way food is both cause of life as well as death; and this all revolves around time, space and causation. So, in a nutshell Anna/food is Brahma—the life giver when digested, and it is death by itself when undigested.

Death is a degenerative force that gives life after a lapse of time under appropriate conditions, so death and life move together. Life and death is lovable, inseparable couple, and without couple there is no force generation. In human system two Kundalini powers exist as couple in unison, which helps each other, one preserves the body and other assists in mergence of the soul with the supernal.

Similarly, God and Yog-Maya, Brahma/God and Maya/illusion, un-manifested and manifested forces, life and death exist in unison and cannot be separated. This is the Srishti/world; and mystery of God and its creation. This is the duality of life and death.

In Sri Vidya, Shiva and Shakti exist for the creation. For dissolution, same Shakti/power turns into the force of Goddess Kali to nullify the creation. So Shakti acts in both ways as the mother of creation, and mother of dissolution. Similarly, there is a same force, which gives life and causes the death. This is the duality of the creation, and the mystery of the unknown.

The most surprising factor is the fear of death in the human mind that makes a human being to love life very intimately; but he does not want to die; this is the Maya/illusion. The knowledge/realization of this duality of life and death is the basis of human's mind evolution; and its churning enriches him with the secret of the unknown that both death and life are one and the same.

One need not love one and hate/dislike other. Both are in continuum, one after the other. Both cannot be disintegrated, distracted, they are always in unison; however neither of one is permanent.

Consciousness and awareness of human mind does not allow him to understand/apprehend this secret of the Almighty. This is the wonder of the Maya/illusion; even great yogis could not penetrate in this secret of Maya/illusion in their consciousness; they just revolved around it without taking the vertical straight upward path to transcend its peripheral boundary.

Only penetration of the consciousness at the Dhahara Chakra can give the enlightenment of the secrets of life and death by the grace of Almighty. One can become the part of Almighty force by integrating and disintegrating his own body in five elements as per His Will.

Yoga can only teach the art of taking away the astral body that can enter to some other body i.e. Pragnya – body. However, the enlightenment from the source light can uplift the Sadhaka to such a high level where he can disintegrate his body in five elements; again he can integrate the body any where in the universe; and thus one can make astral travel by the God's grace.

In the nutshell, it may be visualized that life and death are not separate; they are in unison; they are in continuum one after the other. Breath is the bridge. As the bridge of the breath is collapsed, life disappears and death takes over. Breath discloses this mystery of life and death. One can consciously perceive it having full command on breath.

Discontinuity/void in breaths gives the conscious perception of death in the plane of human existence. This is the wonder of breath in unveiling the mystery of death.

20

Sandhya & Mystery of Void/ Discontinuity and Breath

Evolution starts from Bindu/point. The static/potential energy of Bindu is partially gets converted into the kinetic energy during evolution. Thus, the manifestation continues from the un-manifested static Bindu/point since cosmic energy is in seed form in the Bindu, which is in the un-manifested static stateless state.

By the unknown reasons, Spandau in the Bindu leads to various kinds of intensive throbbing in it, and then part of the Bindu that was static, un-manifested, the manifestation commences in it.

Thus, in the dualist pattern of the Bindu, consisting of manifested and un-manifested parts, out of which the un-manifested part gets manifested and turns into many-ness. Consequently, the creativity pattern by throbbing emerges/comes out of the dielectric in the series one after the other, and multiplying pattern is continued.

The Spandau creates close interaction in the Bindu that leads to throbbing, which generates mysterious force that multiplies within the Bindu/point; and thus the manifestation is continued. This is the origin of the Cosmos from Bindu by Spandau and throbbing.

In fact with out Spandau there cannot be creation and no creativity is feasible. Cosmic Spandau is because of the desire of Almighty. The linkage between various states of the Bindu is through the Spandau; it is not the continued process; it is with discontinuity.

Between manifest state/Sada Shiva/Shiva/Kameshwara and Shakti, and the un-manifested state, there is gap– void—the Kala –the time–the awareness, which always exists. Thus the triangle is formed with time, manifested and un-manifested states.

Without time no transformation takes place. Spandau is Kala –the time. The cosmic throbbing is nothing but time, space and consciousness, which generate the other-ness; and thus the Bindu/ point continues the multiplication.

Initially, unmanifested, Bindu, the Ishwara were existed. By His desires; manifestation; Kameshwara; awareness appeared; and under the effect of Spandau–the Kala–time, the manifestation in many-ness continued.

Kala/time is the division of Absolute; wholeness; one-ness into many-ness. Desire of Absolute is Kama Kala; it is the Maha Maya that created the otherness. Mother of otherness is Kal Mahimani, Nara Hamasi, Lalita, and Chandi and so on.

The initial state of un-manifested i.e. AKAL MANIMANI is changed partially to MAHA MAYA, which is Kali; this is created by the Spandau. Spandau is cosmic dance by Kala/time rhythm that creates manifestation from un-manifested Bindu.

Absolute, the God, measures everything in time frame where as measurement by man is in the material/the Anu form that is the relative knowledge. Time is the evolution, however in the material plane, it is governed by atom. But, time creates material/atom in the Absolute terms under the influence of natural conditions. Particular time is basically termed as Sandhya.

Time of a day where discontinuity or void takes place is termed as Sandhya. There are four Sandhyas in a day. They are Udaya Sandhya (morning by 6 a.m.), Madhya Sandhya (12 noon), Swaimi Sandhya (by 6 p.m.) and the Turiya Sandhya at 12'O clock midnight.

Basically, the gap, when other-ness is likely to approach from the existing state is called Sandhya. This other-ness is Maya/ illusion. As night darkness changes to daylight, the time gap of the dawn is Sandhya. The change to other-ness from the original state is Sandhya. It is called discontinuity/void.

Similarly, as the earth position with respect to sun changes, the changes of seasons occur. There are 12 seasons in year with change of 30-degree position of the earth. That completes one complete cycle in 12 months.

In the same way consciousness (Chaitanya) has four Sandhyas i.e. Jagrik (conscious state) to Swapna (dream state) to Sushupati (deep sleep state) to Turiya (transcendental state) and then to Turiya Tita (the mergence state).

In the same way mind has four Sandhya i.e. mind to Buddhi (intellect) to Chita(consciousness) to Ahankara (ego). The transit gap between thinking and execution of activities by different sections of the mind is Sandhya. The whole world is full of Spandau (gaps), the discontinuities, between the two different states.

Between life and death, there is a gap, the discontinuity, the void; the Spandau; and thus both are the "other-ness" for each other.

This Spandau, the gap, is called the light. In other words this light is time since with time it becomes other-ness and changes. The time that leads to changes is nothing but the cause of evolution. Thus the Spandau that leads to throbbing is the change of evolution and mother of creativity.

Every thing of the manifestation is governed by time; and also the un-manifested to the manifested state revolves around time. Time leads to other-ness; it is Spandau; and when a one-ness change to other-ness is called Sandhya. In simple words, it is nothing but discontinuity—void.

Catching of Sandhya; the time gap of the changes; is the creativity. So creativity is the change of pattern under the influence of Spandau, and it is governed by time. Creativity is the mother of all inventions. Basically, it is in the entrance of void; the gap; and the time; when the change of states is taking place.

The Sandhya is worshiping able Gayatri. It is the direct link with the infinity. It is the light, which transforms the other-ness with time. The contemplation on this light gives all creative ideas related to the deep secrets of the cosmos, which can be manifested and can make wonderful discoveries.

Newton and Einstein could probe into Sandhya/discontinuity/ void, and could catch the essence of creative light for the various discoveries of this nature. The triangle of life and death is completed by the appearance of silence; the Spandau; the gap; the time; the discontinuity; and these are the secret of cosmos.

Breath in and breath out has discontinuity; it is the source of creativity; it is the point of conscious evolution. This discontinuity is required to be extended. Breathing pattern is a source and origin of creativity built in us and this needs to be exploited. Breath in the form of God is always with us and there is no survival without breath/Him.

The individual consciousness to the cosmic consciousness is the Sandhaya that links the soul to the Paramatma/Almighty. This Spandau; the function variation; from relative to the Absolute and vice versa from Absolute to relative is the Sandhya that completes the triangle of soul and Paramatma; it gives the mystery of Self-realization and mergence of soul with the Supernal.

To be aware of this Sandhya; this time gap; reveals the mystery of every thing; but this comes by His grace; efforts and deep understanding. Sandhya links two infinite versions of life and death; also it links soul and Paramatma. To be in other-ness from one-ness through awareness in Sandhya; it is the mystery of the mysteries. From awareness stage to non-awareness stage of Samadhi is the Sandhya. From microcosm to macrocosm is through Sandhya. From awareness of time to the state of timeless-ness is through Sandhya.

The Sandhya completes the triangle to other-ness; and to be with it, is the secret of all the creativities of the Almighty. One has to enter into this gap and who enters is the conqueror of the universal/cosmic secrets.

The state of Samadhi is the mergence of soul with the Supernal through the Sandhya of timeless-ness i.e. shading of awareness. Without Spandau- the time gap, there is no Sandhya. Shiva is the creator of this Spandau, Shakti is the throbbing and time is the energy.

So by interaction of Shiva and Shakti in the Sandhya of time, energy is evolved. It means energy is created through time. In other words energy; the light; is the time. In more subtle form time can create Anu/molecule and Pramanu/atom. Thus time is light.

Light/energy creates matter and vice versa. Matter can create energy. So, energy is Sandhya from the infinity. From time, all types of knowledge are created; it is Paramajyothi. It is Lalita, Parameshwari. Para Gayatri is Absolute; and Apara Gayatri is matter.

Breath is the linkage as time for human evolution; it has to be transcended with discontinuity to be creative in life. This is feasible only by suspending the breath with discontinuity.

In short, time is the miracle of God; it is discontinuity; it is Spandau; Sandhya; light; energy; void and transformation to different matters. And this is the mystery of mysteries of Cosmos, which can be perceived through Sandhya only.

Furthermore, in between the two breaths i.e. out going and the fresh breath, which is on threshold to enter the human system; there exists discontinuity in which one remains without breathe for a fraction of a second. This transient time interval of without breath, between two consecutive breaths, is the span of death; there is no breathing in this interval; one is not in Maya/illusion.

In this interval one is with the spirit/supernal unknowingly. If consciously one can understand and experience this mystery of the divine nature, one can unfold the secret of death, and one can be immensely creative.

Each one of us is the blossom of death about 21600 times per day; the number of times one breaths; however this duration is extremely small. But, if it is integrated considering that one breathes approximately 10 times a minute; taking 6 seconds for each breath with a gap/interval of one second between the two consecutive breaths; then it is not difficult to assess that a person remains nearly 30 minutes without breath per day.

In other words 15-20 hrs per month; about 8-10 days per annum and in total life span of 80 years, about 800 days that is approximately 3% of the life span; he is without breath; he is in void/discontinuity; and thus remains with the death/spirit/ Supernal in totality.

By meditation; by Shunyaka technique; and by consciously observing the breath one can extend this period even up to 10%-15%, and can experience death in this span of life; and can be with the Supernal by his efforts and with the grace of Almighty.

Mind becomes very silent if consciously this time interval is increased without any stress. It can even become the continuum experience to be with the Absolute. This helps to draw direct cosmic energy from the Absolute as and when it is needed by his physical system; gradually his system will be filled with divine light and divine energy.

This is because of the vacuumed created in the system by absence of breath i.e. Maya/illusion, which is filled by divine cosmic energy.

This increases the life span; however, the spiritual aspirant may not have any desire to prolong the life; since for him life is death and death is life; both are same for him. He becomes Jeewan Mukta/liberated soul by the grace of Almighty just by increasing the time interval between two consecutive breaths.

This is the basic mystery of mysteries, and secret of life and death as well as life beyond death. Thus, he can be with the source light of the Absolute; he can step into "Being", and to be beyond time & space.

To be with the source light i.e. with the Supernal is Sandhya. Sandhya is performed at the time of twilight i.e. when night is going to transform in to day light and when day is going to step in to night. This transmigration/transit time interval is termed as Sandhya; the twilight; and Pooja/worship is carried out during this interval.

In terms of yoga it is the time interval between two consecutive breaths when used breath is on the way out from the body; and fresh breath is awaited to enter. This breathless state of microsecond is the natural Sandhya; it is the interval of worship/pooja. This is the span/time interval when life and death are closely knitted; and one is with the Supernal.

An advanced spiritual aspirant can do Sandhya with every breath and can be with the Absolute 21600 times a day. He can draw all the time more and more energy from the cosmos. Thus, Sandhya becomes continuum with time for him.

This may become even without awareness; and Sadhaka/spiritual aspirant may experience the blessings of Samadhi being with the divine light and enjoying the nectar of divinity.

So Sandhya is not the ritual of worship as generally being performed; but it is the yogic mergence with the Supernal by worshipping and extending the interval between the consecutive breaths. This is from Sri Vidya, which is the mother of all the religions. This brings a spiritual aspirant to the stage of enlightenment that is the source knowledge, and beyond this no knowledge is required.

This gives light to the soul by mergence with Supernal; and then one is beyond time, space and causation. One becomes silent and experiences complete silence within him self; he gets the full glimpses of death being alive and is enlightened.

In this transcendental state mind, intellect and consciousness disappear and merges with soul; and soul merges with the cosmic consciousness. This is the fundamental science of microcosm; and all others are only the applied sciences.

Enlightenment brings the knowledge of fundamental science i.e.: knowledge of secret of death; permanent/absolute silence; super consciousness; elongation of life span; migration to the better world after death; and so on.

Furthermore astral body after death, travel towards Vasu Loka, and then to Rudra Loka. In Vasu Loka astral body is given opportunity to shed vices, to improve, and if succeeded then it is allowed to go to Rudra Loka by the master spirit/Almighty.

In this Loka if astral body becomes pure and totally desire less, then as pure soul it is qualified to go to Aditya Loka. Here the soul is liberated from the cycles of birth and death and merges with the Supernal. Later, if required by Almighty, this pure soul is sent as an Avatar/incarnation to Bhu Loka—in this world. Thus, Jeevatma gets salvation by the austerities, and blessings of the omnipresent, omnipotent and omniscient energy source—the Almighty.

In addition, there are namely two Margas/ways for Self-realization namely Dhum Raj Marga and Achi Raja Marga/Aditya Marga. Dhum Raj Marga is the ritualistic path, the path of earning Puniya and Dharma etc. It is the path of Skama. Aditya Marga is the path of Nishkama. It is the path of worship of light without any Sankalpa/thoughts/desires.

This is the supreme path, expressed by Yama to Nichiketa who disclosed him the secrets of death. This is the direct path of mergence with Supernal without any Sankalpa.

In this path, the breath is to be suspended and gap between breaths needs to be extended; then only brain chemical is formed beyond the bio-spiritual atoms or from the cosmos energy brain cells are activated; and then only one recollects his past births and this discloses the mystery of death; life beyond death; and continuation of life after life.

Furthermore, with this one enters in the time-less zone; he is beyond time & space; in this discontinuity of mergence with cosmic consciousness, he becomes whole; here energy is trapped, which gives him long life, health and happiness.

Thus, the whole universe becomes miracle of breath for him provided he has full command on breath; he lives in breath; and he becomes breath.

21

Dhyana/Meditation by Witnessing the Breath

What is Dhyana/Meditation? It is very complex to explain. This is because in meditation, one is not there then how it can be explained what it is? When some one is totally merged in meditation; in self; and then he becomes totally unaware.

If one is aware it means he is not in Dhyana/meditation. Then he is a separate identity; he is observing the happenings within and without; he is then merely a spectator and not in meditation. Under such conditions one is not within it. This may be termed as awakening meditation.

And if one is within it then only he loses his identity. That is the real meditation; then he is beyond time; he is merged in Absolute—the Supernal.

Conscious meditation/Jagrik Turiya/awakening transcendental state is not the ultimate of meditation. What any body talks or try to define is only the conscious state; it is the state of Dyana/ meditation with awareness.

It is the starting junction of meditation; and most of us end meditation at this junction only even after life long practice. One gets only marginal benefit out of such meditation; it is meditation with awareness/consciousness.

Furthermore, if one continuous meditation then with number of discontinuities, one gets experience of unconscious/unaware mediation; he crosses the boundary of time & space; he is then in timeless era i.e. Akaal, which is the abode of "Being". This is the ultimate meditation; this is called Turiya-Tita. It is beyond transcendental; beyond consciousness; it is conscious-less mergence state with discontinuity.

When one comes out from this unconscious meditation, his personality gets modulated. If it is continued couple of times then there occurs transformation in his personality; he is then filled with divine virtues and divine energy. This energy is helpful for his overall well-being and extension of his life with perfect health and happiness.

All the preparations needed for meditation are highlighted here. First and foremost is Dhyana Bumika/preface of meditation; one needs to learn this from a self realized Guru/master. Basically process of meditation starts by witnessing the breath and being with the discontinuity of breath in and breathe out.

Extension of this discontinuity/void gives immense energy for meditation and to remain with the self. Through this energy one needs to concentrate on Triputi junction i.e. the point between eyebrows; and even for this some basic preparations are required.

The followings are the basic prerequisites before starting the meditation; various techniques and multiple inner most experiences:

1. On the physical plane, the body must be healthy. Stomach must be empty/not fully loaded. It means the best time for meditation is morning and evening hours. But at least there must be 4-5 hours gaps between the food intake and the meditation.

2. Inner system of the Dhyani/meditator must be healthy in all respects. Before starting meditation some breathing exercises must be done to feel fully relaxed. These can be forceful breathing exercises basically using Shunyaka technique, Kriya yoga and so on; so that Udana Prana is well generated in the system. Basically breath is the gate way to meditation.

3. All past thoughts from the mind must be removed. One must learn to live in present. What is "now", it is the every thing. One must consider that past is dead and future is uncertain.

No fear for future to be kept in mind. He must think that he is the lord of present. Since one can use only present and can command it as he wishes?

No need to brood on past. Projection of past only creates confusion. Generally one wastes most of his life time to be living and thinking of past only. One must attend/check even smallest appearance of thoughts in the present before meditation so that it should not manifest in due course.

4. The place of sitting for meditation must be comfortable. Meditator must face east, or west or north. Outer noise must be the minimum around the sitting space and circulation of fresh air shall be adequate. It is better if plants, green curtains are around and environment is natural. Seashore, bank of the river, water tank and plants/trees around give much inspiration to the Meditator and add to his inner peace.

5. Meditation is a psychosomatic exercise so the inner peace, outer calmness and peaceful environment help to evolve the Meditator.

6. The best preparation for meditation is equivalent to the 2/3 of the achievement. After well preparation, Meditator must chant the Mantra and be attentive at the Triputi/in between the eyebrows. This is gross awareness stage.

Later Meditator must close eyes, remember his Guru/master, Ishtdevata and switch on from gross Mantra recitation to the Mona/silent Japa. This gradually brings the gross stage to the subtle stage to the Meditator with the conscious awareness. This is the second Bhumika for the meditation.

7. In third Bhumika, Meditator must start Kriya yoga without chanting the Mantra. This gives rise to awareness of Prana in the system. This yoga paditi/system is known as Raj yoga. If the Prana is evolved, the progress in yoga becomes very fast.

On the contrary if there is mal-functioning of various Pranas in the system, different stomach problems start originating, and success in yoga/ meditation becomes difficult.

The Meditator must take immense care for correct/adequate distribution of various Pranas in the system by breathing exercises and self-management. Breath plays significant constructive role in meditation.

8. Human body is microcosm and cosmos is macrocosm. The Udana Prana/life force is generated in the microcosm; on traveling through Sushumna Nadi of the spinal cord passing through different chakras, it reaches to Ajna chakra; and then to Chida akasha; and gradually getting transformed into light, which merges with the Supernal.

When Udana Prana reaches trinity, awareness of breath diminishes and gradually awareness of Prana is loosened. This state is known as CHATUR YAGA KAMMA. This happens in gradual steps from awakening to dream state to DRUG/SUSHUPATI state.

In this state Meditator is not aware of breath and not of Mantra recitation. It is half conscious mixed Bhumika state. Also, Jeeva— the personal soul is released from the divine soul gradually, if Jeevatma—personal soul ascends to this level along with it. Finally, partially pure divine soul remains at this junction.

It is half or semi mergence state just above the Tirupati. Half of the awakening consciousness is lost at this level. Further to this NISHKARIYA BOOMIKA state is reached when Jeeva/living being's conscious awareness merges into pure soul completely. No more minds' existence is left here; it is the functionless state.

Life force/Prana merges with soul and Meditator starts getting cosmic consciousness and his third eye is gradually opened after years of such practice by the grace of Almighty.

9. Meditator is still conscious. His conscious is not yet released. This happens at the Ajna chakra. This is the Kutakash Chaitnaya state. After this stage, transformation of light occurs from Udana Prana and life force. With the appearance of light and its ascendance to Chida Akasha there is no more time, space consciousness. It is the state of universal oneness.

Meditator starts considering all human being are alike and he inherently develops state of universal brother hood by its own in this state.

He then develops divine qualities/virtues of forgiveness, love, renunciation, no hatred, humility, truthfulness and like these 27 qualities is developed as described by Lord Krishna in Gita for a divine spiritual aspirant; as He Himself being perfect in all these qualities. This is the conscious Turiya/transcendental state. It is the state of monistic dualism but not the state of mergence in the sky.

10. As the light further ascends to the Chida akasha. It crosses the state of TIRUPATI BHANGA, where there is; no time; no space; and no consciousness; it is the state of mergence. All the three identities time, space and consciousness become one. As this pure light further ascends, it reaches UNMANI, where it spreads and awareness is lost. This is VIDHEHA STATE of evolution.

11. Finally when it reaches Sahasara, it becomes center of source light. Meditator enters in the state of Samadhi at Sahasara. And to the Apex center when this ascends, it blesses to the Meditator the glimpses of Para Samadhi. Moment this divine light merges with the macro cosmos, spiritual aspirant is in the state of Nirvikalpa Samadhi; he is beyond "time & space'.

This is the state of void with discontinuity.

Furthermore, as this light returns back to Ajna and subsequently to Muladhara chakra, it gives the blessings and experience of Svikalpa Samadhi to the Meditator/Dhayani. All this happens with discontinuities. Thus, with this Meditator achieves "nothing" but every thing besides manifestation of consciousness.

The above explains preparation for meditation and intrinsic evolution, which only meditator can perceive, conform and visualize; all this is mysterious secrets of secrets.

Apart from the above, some times one does not feel vital energy in the body due to various reasons. In such situation, one must stiff hands, legs and complete body, couple of times and then relaxes. In this process of stiffness and relaxation of different parts of the body, muscles of body get energized.

Even to do this perfect breath control is needed. Without breath regulation, energy cannot be generated in the muscles. Since breath is God; and meditation intrinsically moves around breath.

Sometimes divine dance and physical exercise is needed to energize the system; and by due relaxation this energy is transferred to inner system.

This energy, when experienced in the system, must be transferred virtually and mentally to Muladhara chakra before the meditation process is started. With these exercises meditation becomes effort-less.

Basically in the discontinuity between stiffness and relaxation period immense energy is appeared that is the inner most significant energy, which can be easily used for meditation and it is transformed for the purpose to step into "Being" to transcendence of "space & time" for manifestation of consciousness.

At this stage, one must be conscious of breath very deeply. He must be fully conscious of discontinuity between two consecutive breaths. Gradually, this discontinuity is increased. Finally, a stage comes, when breath gets suspended; finally, breath gets disappeared by itself. This brings the conscious-less stage of mergence. It comes and goes with discontinuity.

This is the ultimate stage of meditation. This enriches the aspirant/sadhaka with subtle virtues and divine qualities. All these subtle virtues bring unique transformation in his life.

In fact breath is a secret of this achievement and realization.

22

Awakening of Kundalini Power Through Breath and Prana

To understand the awakening of Kundalini, overall perception of Breath and Pranas is required. There are five types of elemental Prana in a human body. As the air/ Pawan by the process of breathing goes through the nostrils inside the human system, it gets converted into Shavas/breath at the Visuddhi chakra. This breath after taking the energy from the soul at the Dhahara chakra is converted into Prana. However, only a part of the breath is transformed into Prana.

This Prana is further transformed to Samana, Vayana, Apana and Udana Pranas. By the close interaction and impact of various Pranas, Udana Prana is formed. It has maximum of sky content and only this Prana can ascend through chakras. It is transformed into the divine light after perfect/partial purification in the different chakras of the human system before it reaches at the Ajna chakra. Udana Prana is Brahman/divine.

On the contrary, other Pranas are manifestation of Maya/ illusion for the Jeevatma. They contain more percentage of earth, water, fire and air contents. Only Udana Prana is full of ether; it can take sky ness path for mergence with Supernal after transformation in divine light on the ascending path through various chakras.

Basically by the yoga practices and self efforts, Udana Prana is generated in the human system. There are two processes: first is by Puraka, Rechaka and Kumbhaka practices of controlled breathing processes of yoga; by such breathing transformation of Udana Prana takes place from the existing Pranas.

Second process is: by two Pranas namely Prana and Vayana like Pandvas being on upper side, above the navel in the human system; where as Samana and Apana like Kauravas being on the lower side, below the navel center; the close interaction and impact of these Pranas like the Kurkshetra war leads to generate the light out of their mutual rubbing; and thus Udana Prana is generated.

Practically, to generate the Udana Prana, one must breathe through the stomach, concentrating on naval centre. Gradually with time, one will get sensation of Udana Prana. However, this will be achieved by divine practices besides the blessings of God. This generated divine light is named as Udana Prana i.e. life force.

On the other hand, as Kauravas and Pandvas are born by the supreme Will of Lord Krishna, so other four Prana except Udana Prana are born by the soul light existing at the Dhahara/Anahata chakra.

Also, Udana Prana/light is the outcome/effect of interaction of these Pranas. However, the basic cause of appearance of Udana Prana is the soul (consciousness/force/part of Almighty) residing in the human system.

The close interaction of these Pranas separates Udana Prana automatically. This function is independent by itself as the out come of the close action less action of the different Pranas.

This Udana Prana immediately after its appearance interacts with Swadhisthanam chakra, being nearest to navel center. Also, by the warmth/ fire/Agni effect of Manipura, which is the closed chakra to Swadhisthanam; Udana Prana is purified and absorbed by the awareness of fire/Agni.

Thus, the flame of fire, containing Udana Prana spreads all around and interacts with Muladhara chakra being closest to Manipura and Swadhisthanam. The Kundalini power lying as three and half inch coiled in coccyx near Muladhara, in a Samadhi state, is then awakened by the heat and light of Udana Prana.

The Kundalini power lies in transcended and dormant state under the effect of Maya/illusion until and unless it is pushed by the force of the Udana Prana. As it is pushed; it rises like a snake, which was resting in 3 ½ inches turns coils from coccyx under Muladhara, and then goes to Manipura chakra through the Swadhisthanam along with the light/energy of Udana Prana.

In this chakra under the effect of water of Swadhisthanam, Kundalini power tends to become Sattvik; it gets purified like Mani/diamond and cools down.

Further, kundalini power along with Udana Prana/life force that got converted partially into the divine light ascends to Dhahara chakra. The interaction of ascending energy at the Dhahara and Manipura chakras continue gradually; and finally the divine light of Udana Prana and Kundalini is absorbed by the soul residing at Dhahara.

As a pure soul light from Dhahara chakra, this energy ascends to Visuddhi and Lambika chakras. Residual Prana remaining with this energy loses its Pranic function at Visuddhi chakra.

Other ingredient of light i.e. yellow, blue, red etc., are filtered in the Lambika chakra, and purest of the pure divine light ascends to the Ajna chakra. Here there is no Udana Prana, no Kundalini and no other gradients remain; all are merged in oneness in the pure divine light of the soul. No duality remains here; all duality is disappeared.

If soul has carried along with it Jeeva, i.e. as Jeevatma/ personalized soul; then there are chances of mental vision and memories at the Ajna chakra due to the presence of Jeeva/living being; since there is not only the exclusive light of the Atman/ soul. It means Jeeva (as Jeevatma) has ascended to this location along with the pure soul/Atman from the Dhahara chakra.

If there is pure soul then the Atman Sakshatkara i.e. Self-realization is possible at this location since it is the stage of the opening of third eye. However, Self-realization gradually starts manifesting/ reflecting in the Sadhaka's awareness with time if this practice is continued for years under by the blessings of

Master; and then one can transcendent time and space, and takes step into "Being".

Under these conditions breath is very feeble and suspended. It can be said that breath exists as life force and moves up and down through spinal cord. However, total disappearance of breath occurs in those moments when one is fully beyond time and space.

From the Ajna chakra, light spreads in the Chida akasha/ Gagana and Sadhaka experiences awakening/dream/deep slumbering/Sushupati/ and then Turiya/transcendence Sandhya states. In presence of the Jeeva, there prevails superfine awareness; but if Jeeva is separated and only soul/Atman ascends; then there does not remain any awareness.

It is called the Turiya state/transcendental state; then state of Turiya tita i.e. mergence with Supernal is unknowingly experienced. This is the highest achievement of human life; there is nothing beyond this.

Turiya is the blissful state. However, Illusion/Maya of bliss is different than that of the blissful state. In this blissful state there is no ego; no Kundalini; no Prana; no Jeeva; and only there is the presence of pure soul that gives the divine light. So, blissful state is a state of mergence of pure light with Supernal. Only at this stage soul is liberated. No function is required to be performed in the stage.

It is state of Turiya Tita, which is beyond Turiya/transcendence state. No one can describe this state. If one can describe and say, it means he was in Maya/illusion and not in mergence; in Turiya Tita; and in blissful state.

Here in this stage, the conscious transforms into unconsciousness/conscious-less; and no one can describe what happened; it is beyond time & space; universal consciousness and human consciousness merge with discontinuities in non local pattern; separateness disappears.

This is the state when a human being becomes God like. He and he become the same.

However, consciousness is manifested when it come back to usual conscious state from this unconscious/conscious-less state with divine healing energy, which enhances longevity and well-being.

The above clarifies the role of Breath, Pranas, Kundalini, Jeevatma, Jeeva and soul in subtle manner in the spiritual evolution of a Sadhaka/spiritual aspirant.

Furthermore, before a Sadhaka takes up the practices of yoga, all the Chakras in his system are closed/sealed. Every Chakra has its original characteristics. When the chakras are blossom by the passage of Kundalini power and Udana Prana, specific dormant tendencies of a Sadhaka awake in the process.

As the Kundalini power in the subtle stage of Samadhi resting in the coccyx at Muladhara region as the three and half-inch coil awakens by the immense pressure of Udana Prana and its heat energy, it then tries to pierce through Muladhara Chakra and gradually ascends through Swadhisthana Chakra.

The entire earth bound concealed tendencies become active in the mind of a beginner/ Sadhaka. Earth bound tendencies like sex/procreation, attraction for varieties of tasty food, greed, anger, pride and attachments etc., manifest to the highest level depending on the potentiality of the tendencies.

Some times Sadhaka is not able to control the manifested urge that forces him to indulge in these activities through the lowest possible level. He becomes Deha abhimani/proud of physical body and profoundly gets attached with instinctual desires to fulfill them.

But, gradually, if he continues his Sadhana/spiritual practices, these tendencies die down. And Sadhaka gets further purified as the Udana Prana passes under the fire of Manipura and Swadhisthana chakras, and approaches to other higher chakras.

However, this stage of initial evolution is very dangerous and one can become prey of negative tendencies for a long time till their effect is subsided with time. One has to be much disciplined in thoughts, words and deeds in life. Moreover he needs to lead a pious life with full awareness. Being in awareness, effect of negative tendencies gets dissolved.

Furthermore, to overcome negative tendencies, transformation of physical body vibration can be modulated by proper breathing process to enhance evolution. Breath plays a very significant role to dilute the negative mental tendencies as one passes through the evolution stage.

As the time passes and if the Sadhaka/spiritual aspirant continues his Sadhana with sincerity, he may become the master of eight Sidhis of yoga that make him Mahatma, the great soul with time for the external world. Inside, his Jeevatma gets purified and he passes comfortably from the four stages of evolution i.e. he may transcend easily Wakeful stage, Dream, Sushupati and Turiya/ transcendental State and finally he may step into Savikalpa to Nirvikapa Samadhi.

He becomes one with the divine light in the Turiya state before mergence with the Supernal. In the process of evolution he becomes Sthiita Pragnya. He gets evolved more in divine activities that project his inherent talents but his talents don't show his egoism of any kind.

On the contrary, in the initial stages of evolution when energies are mostly concentrated in Muladhara and Swadhisthanam; he has mixed instinct and free nature; his consciousness is also mixed.

Depending on the mental tendency and variable mixed ideas in his consciousness, the decisions he takes of life, may prove to be self contradictory with time. At this stage he is more under the effect of Maya, the illusion; his nature will be very transient.

His nature may be Tamasic, Rajasik or Sattvik; his behavior is unpredictable even for himself in the initial stages. His actions may not show consistency since all his actions are governed by the invoked tendencies in the lower charkas. He may himself be surprised for his own behavior sometimes being Sattvik and sometimes highly Tamasik. This is because of the transient stage of evolution.

Sometimes such a beginner aspirant talks of himself and may talk futile. His actions cannot be predicated unless his Udana Prana stabilizes in the Manipura and Dhahara chakras.

In the beginning he is SKAMA SADHAKA and follows subtle ego path; he can curse to the fellow beings with prejudices and Raga to fulfill his own worldly desires. But, gradually as he ascends in the path of spirituality, he becomes desire less. He becomes NISHKAMA SADHAKA.

Furthermore, as he enjoys to be with himself and to be near to his soul as much as possible; then his action supersedes cause and effect. He gets fused in himself as if two different qualities of milks are mixed together, which then cannot be separated. Thus, he supersedes his bad desires and even he does not show/project any caliber, which he posses. He gradually becomes sober, mindfulness and awakens all the time.

As he climbs up in the path of vertical journey, he needs to control his mind by Dhayana. Tranquil breath needs to be generated and regulated breath need to be observed; also, witnessing of the breath is to be practiced. He is neither to negate his own mind and nor to provoke it. By this his mind becomes strong.

Furthermore, gradually he trains his mind with positive thoughts and follows philosophy of the art of correct living and dealings. He trains his mind to explain that desires of any kind is futile; death waits at the doorstep, which gives him perfect peace; he expands awareness to infuse detachment; he contemplates on the satisfaction and dissatisfaction. He thanks God for all His mercy on him.

By this way, if mind is trained, it becomes one pointed and this is all needed for prelude to Dhyana for the forward vertical journey so that ego, subconscious, and desires do not become obstacles in the path of spiritual evolution.

Thus, a Sadhaka in the path of evolution at the Swadhisthana and Muladhara can train his mind initially so that ego gets dissolved; and attitudes towards desires become nullified and their futility is understood. So that onward journey becomes natural throughout till the mergence takes place.

In short, miseries during initial evolution are natural under the effect of Maya and latent tendencies. Guyana/knowledge is required to develop the conscious attitude so that the problems are tolerated as the natural phenomenon. Grace of Almighty does help to the real Sadhakas in this path.

Prayers are the divine boon to the Sadhakas to come out from such obstacles, which is the best possible way to take up this onward journey for mergence with the Supernal; and to be beyond time & space. Breath is the selfless companion under all conditions.

Any time one turns his consciousness towards his breathe, he will be in touch with miraculous powers to assist him to take his divine journey. To be with the breath is like to be in "Being".

23

Evolution Through Kriya Yoga–The Regulated Breathing Process

Evolution is the basic purpose of existence of human being. For this life force/Udana Prana/spiritual energy is needed; and it is required to be generated in the human system by self efforts. Kriya yoga is an advance technique for self realization and evolution in life in shortest span through life force energies.

Kriya yoga is sacred dormant regulated breathing practice. Disciples learn this technique from the Masters after they become sufficiently advance in spiritual practices. It is not healthy to practice without sufficient guidance and also until one is not spiritually well prepare to take up this advance technique for self realization.

It is not proper to high light this technique so that it should not be mis-utilised and become harmful to the practitioners. So, only evolution through Kriya yoga shall be brought in this chapter.

By the grace of "Being" in the process of Yoga Sadhana, Udana Prana can be generated. The Udana Prana is later called or named as life force. After its appearance by the years of sincere practice, it passes through the Muladhara chakra via coccyx and gradually ascends through the spinal cord through Sushumna Nadi to the Ajna chakra.

It passes after piercing through Swadhistanam, Manipura, Dhahara/Anahata, Visuddhi and Lambika chakra; finally it/life force get settled at the Ajna chakra, which is Kutakasha Chaitanya center. It is located in between the eyebrows.

Life force energy gets concentrated gradually at this center/ chakra. It is two pedals chakra. Here at this chakra, life force either can take vertical path or take the backward path to the Muladhara. It is very important center. It is gateway to Chida Akasha, and also the highest center for monitoring and controlling the horizontal plane activities.

By the self-efforts and Guru/master's directions, one can ascend the life force at this level. Above this is the pathless sky path; life force/light move itself through Braham Nadi towards this path by the direction of cosmic force, which is beyond time & space.

At this chakra, after deep concentration, on passing through Awakening, Dreamy, Slumbering/Susupati and Transcendence/ Turiya stages, the life force gets transformed into the Cosmic divine light; it ascends through vertical sky path through Brahamnadi to the Chida Akasha gradually.

On passing through the nine different chakras on this sky-ness path in the Chida Akasha, it reaches to Unmani chakra before piercing through Sahasrara chakra on the way to the mergence with the Supernal; thus it transcendences time and space.

However, if the life force cannot transform in to divine light due to various unforeseen reasons, it takes the downward journey from the Ajna chakra back to the Muladhara passing through Lambika, Visuddhi, Dhahra, Manipura and Swadhistanam charkas. Sometimes with the fastest speed it reaches to its starting origin i.e. Muladhara.

Sometimes, it looks as if through astral plane the life force has descended back to Muladhara. It can also ascend through the astral plane from Muladhara for the advance Sadhakas. For the life force to follow the vertical sky-ness path depends on the evolution of the Sadhaka/aspirant and his years of long practice along with the grace of the Almighty.

During descend the life force is likely to follow the same backward path; and thus it completes the one round of revolution in the human system from Muladhara to Ajna chakra, and Ajna to Muladhara.

Again by the presence of lively Prana in the life force, and by deep mental inward concentration or by the advanced breathing exercise of the Kriya yoga, it can again ascends/climbs up through the spinal cord like a serpent via Sushumna Nadi, and on passing through the various charkas, it reaches with the least resistance up to the Ajna Chakra.

It stays there for a few seconds; and during this time Sadhaka enjoys the presence of Shakti at the Kutaksha Chaitanya center/Ajna chakra before it takes the backward descend path.

The mind of the Sadhaka with this process of the up and down movement of life force gets fully inward engrossed within the life force; and its upward and downward movement in the spinal cord is witnessed by the engrossed mind.

By repetition of this process again and again in the spinal cord, the Sadhaka/spiritual aspirant experiences that the total energy of the system is concentrated in spinal cord particularly in the Sushumna Nadi; and quanta of energy is moving up and down between Muladhara and Ajna; and back following the same path.

In this way, Sadhaka feels that all other major system of the body including heart, lungs etc. are fully relaxed during this process since the energy has been withdrawn from the entire system; and it has got concentrated in the vertical spinal column.

Entire system is then basically Jada and Achetan/unconscious state for the Sadhaka for the outward/worldly happenings around him since the energy from all the five senses have been withdrawn. Sadhaka is not even aware of various physical happenings around him.

Under these conditions /status, there is no energy with the ears, eyes, nose, skin and tongue, and the master of senses—the mind is engrossed and enjoying the movement of the energy in the spinal cord.

This is basically the stateless state of the Sadhaka; his mind is still, and it is in a horizontal plane up to the level of Ajna chakra; he is in a state of full relaxation.

In this state, no physical movement of any part of the body is taking place; and complete system is stand still; except auto system of the body, which is in the working mode; and complete energy of the entire system is concentrated in the Sushumna Nadi.

Mind is in the thoughtless and silence state; but it is in conscious State with the inward awareness of the pranic life force energy.

As the life force travels up and down through the Sushumna Nadi, it magnetizes the Sushumna Nadi since life force is an Udana Prana—a concentrated quanta of the pranic spiritual energy.

Its repeated up and down movement through the Sushumna generates the electro-static energy on its tiny walls; and gradually the walls of Sushumna Nadi becomes magnetized since the Sadhaka during Yoga Sadhana is insulated from the feeble magnetic fields of the earth by insulating himself from the ground by using the insulated carpet/cloth on which he sits for meditation.

Once the Sushumna Nadi is fully magnetized, the magnetic charge energy gets transmitted to the spinal cord by mutual induction process, and thus, the spinal cord gets magnetized.

Since sun and moon nadis (Ida and Pingala) are the important parts of spinal cord and are housed in it and are around Sushumna Nadi, also get magnetized during this process along with the other Nadis of the spinal cord. In this way each and every cell of the spinal cord gets magnetized.

Gradually, number of spiritually magnetized cells increases; and also the concentration of intensity of spiritual magnetic charge on each cell get manifested by up and down flow of life force energy in the Sushumna Nadi.

As this process goes on, sun and moon Nadis after getting fully charged act as the main source for the distribution of spiritual charge energy to the entire system by the process of breath in and breathe out.

This is because of the fact that these Nadis are closely linked with the breathing system and breathing process. How the breathing system functions inside the human body in distribution of accumulated subtle spiritual energy to each cell, it is very complex to perceive. Presently it is beyond perception to explain.

It is well known that oxygen and pranic energy get distributed to each and every cell of the human system; and thus spiritual energy also gets distributed through this process as the reserve of charge of magnetic spiritual energy increases in sun and moon nadis of the system.

Gradually, by years of practice of revolution of life energy through the spinal cord, each and every cell of the body retained the charge of spiritual pranic energy.

Minimum 12 to 20 years of sincere practice may make the Sadhaka to be fully spiritual by body, mind and intellect. His thoughts, words and deeds will become fully spiritual. This in turn increases the mind's spiritual energy and turns the Sadhaka a spiritual enlightened Yogi. However, it cannot happen without the blessings of infinite omnipresent force, the Almighty.

This is a process, but all this is possible by His grace since Maya—illusion will try to take him back to square one again and again. But he must get up again and again and walk likes a child until he/she learns how to walk alone without a support. One has to live with light of the self to be healthy and happy.

By the above practice, the body of the Sadhaka gets charged gradually with time, and even an ordinary person can feel the certain amount of feeble voltage if naked body of Sadhaka is just touched.

In short, circulation of life force in the spinal cord of the Sadhaka/spiritual aspirant turns him gradually to a perfect yogi who develops all the occult powers in due course of time.

Pramahansa Yogananda Ji has clearly mentioned in his spiritual realization discourses that one round of circulation of life force through all the chakras in the spinal cord gives an evolution of one year in life, which one achieves by proper and right spiritual living during this period.

This means that by perfect spiritual living of one year by thoughts, words and deeds, the amount of spiritual energy, which

Sadhaka accumulates in the system, one round of travel of life force from Muladhara chakra to Ajna chakra and back renders the same amount of spiritual energy to the system; however, one round of this travel of life force just takes a few microseconds.

Thus, Kriya Yoga and revolution of one round of life force through the system leads the accelerated evolution to a devotee/ Sadhaka so that in his life span itself, he can be self realized soul; he can achieve mergence with the Supernal and may attained Savikalpa and then Nirvikalpa Samadhi in due course with out any restrains.

This quickens the evolution process and one becomes spiritually realized in this birth; he can become Jeewan Mukta/ liberated soul by the grace of Almighty, which otherwise would have taken several uncounted births.

The above as discussed, is the benefit of the ascending and descending of the life force in the spinal cord in the human system. No other process can render such benefits and make an ordinary human being a self realized soul in his life span.

What is basically required for this highest achievement in one's own life span is burning devotion, immense patience, rigid desire/ sankalpa and above all Guru's grace and kindness & blessings of the Almighty to transcendence of time & space.

Without the appearance of life force in the system, it is not possible to enhance the consciousness.

By the energy of life force and its free flow takes the human consciousness beyond time & space; it becomes easy to be within and one can transcendence consciousness to be in conscious-less state with discontinuities; and thus evolution is enhanced and consciousness is manifested, which effects life span and overall well-being.

This is the miracle of Kriya yoga, which is well established spiritual science of regulated breathing. Kriya yoga in nutshell revolves around breath. Hence breath is God; one cannot be self realized without the command of breath. One must adore breath; worship it; breath is life.

24

Transcendence of Time & Space by Breath

All the techniques of Dhyana/meditation are the perfect techniques to step in to "Being" and "transcendence of time & space". One must perfect one of the techniques and follow it regularly; he will gradually succeed to the path of Self-realization, and will be able to step into "Being". All the techniques lead to mergence; and are for "to be beyond time & space".

In meditation there are no mind and not even divisible mind; mind is annihilated; no time concept; and no awareness, but awareness/consciousness exists with discontinuity, which leads to the oneness with the cosmos. No disintegration and separateness – total oneness with the cosmic awareness; and to become one with that Supreme power is the final achievement by following one of meditational techniques.

Transcendence of time and space in meditation takes place. This is because of the fact that mind is annihilated in meditation then mind is not aware of time. If Sadhaka/aspirant in meditation is fully engrossed, track of time is disappeared. When he comes back to consciousness then only he detects the unnoticed time lapse; it shows that he was in "Akaal" i.e. beyond time; in other words time was transcended in meditation; he was beyond time.

Under these conditions, mind was thoughtless; mind was annihilated; there were no thoughts of any kind in mind. It means there was no space to move thoughts in the mind. Thoughts move in mind since mind has memory of past and mind dreams of future.

Being in present during meditation, space gets restricted for movement of thoughts.

In present, for single in coming and out going breath, there is restricted space for movement of thoughts. This shows that when breath is suspended in present in meditation; or breath is very feeble; it does not have space for flow of thoughts. So, the space is too transcended in meditation.

So, in meditation, when mind is annihilated, it shows there are no thoughts; flow of thoughts has been suspended; mind, buddhi (intellect), consciousness and ahankara have been merged. Thus, space for movement in mind is temporary collapsed; so time and space are transcended in meditation.

There are various meditation techniques; but, three techniques in general are followed; namely: AUM technique; Gayatri Sandhya; and Udana Prana/ Life Force Technique. All these techniques are closely revolve around breath. Here intrinsic philosophy of meditation in the light of science, as conceived, has been highlighted.

The following must be perceived deeply:

1.0 Ahankara and Chitta/ consciousness to become integral is the basic and foremost requirement, however both must be manifested with subtle divine virtues. Particularly, Ahankara is the motivation and decision-making faculty, and Chita/consciousness is the logical base; and these are the pro and cons of the decision-making faculty.

One has mind, buddhi (intellect), Chitta (consciousness) and Ahankara before action is undertaken; and even after the action has been executed. After action there can be reaction in mind and intellect. Chitta – the consciousness can manifest the reaction. Ahankara is the manifested consciousness; and may be divisible; or integrated consciousness; it depends on the reaction of mind and intellect after the action.

2.0 All the above four constituents: mind; intellect; consciousness; and ego; give the various capabilities to a human being. Mind revolves around the Ichha Shakti. It revolves around the desires; their creation; ways and means; so as to fulfill all of them.

Buddhi/intellect and Chitta/consciousness revolve around Guyana/knowledge. With accumulation of knowledge, help/assistance is rendered to accomplish desires created by mind; where as Ahankara/egoism is the Kriya; the final action taken to execute the activity to fulfill desires.

Without Aham/ego—self, activity cannot be undertaken. Although activity has been desired, knowledge is gathered but without the force of Aham/ego – self of the Jeeva, it cannot be put into action to accomplish. Furthermore, it must be understood that mind is atomic in nature, and it is very subtle and mutative.

The silence cannot enter into the mind easily unless mind becomes greatest and enters into super conscious state. The moment it enters in the super conscious state, awareness goes/disappears; no more existence of mind remains; and only silence prevails. So when there is silence; there is no mind; mind is annihilated; no awareness remains.

It is stateless state of being super conscious; and without consciousness and awareness. It is intuitive state; divine state of Svikalpa Samadhi; and one cannot remain there for a long duration. This state may come and go; this is the state with discontinuity. How it comes and goes? It is only the play of Almighty; it is a play of time & space.

In this state, physical microcosm merges into macrocosm of the cosmos. This integrity is the stateless state of Samadhi; beyond time & space; if prolonged, it becomes non-return state to the awareness; it is then called Nirvikalpa Samadhi; a state of total non-returned mergence. Generally, it happens at the time of death.

3.0 Sandhya Gayatri is the technique, which leads to take Sadhaka up to this stage of mergence beyond time & space by gradual suspension of breath; mind then becomes un-mutative for a long time by just keeping Dhyana/attention on the incoming and outgoing breath.

As Dhyana is continued, time comes when breath get suspended as the gap between incoming and outgoing breaths increases; Sadhaka is then with the spirit during this increased interval/gap; this finally leads to an un-mutative stage of mind since mind gets its energy from breath only.

This develops the mind and raises it to the unaware and unconscious stage, which is beyond Maya/illusion; thus silence and super consciousness, intuition, the stateless state, just pour in gradually by Almighty's grace; it is the state beyond time & space; a state of "Being".

This is the achievement by Sandhya Gayatri Sadhana similar to the other techniques. Furthermore, it can be said that by negation of mind, Buddhi (intellect), Chitta (conscious) and Ahankara/ego, one is near to soul.

Added to this if consciousness is also diminished during meditation, there is ascend of soul to higher centers; and its mergence occurs with the Supernal. One steps in to "Being"; to be beyond time & space. This is the state of unison of microcosmic consciousness to the macrocosmic consciousness. Then there is no ego remains. Ego gets totally nullified and disappeared.

In other words in this stage mind, consciousness and ego are in unison; it is the disappearance state; it is the state of mergence with Supernal. This is state beyond feeling and of any action; it is the state of "Being". In this stage consciousness is manifested with divine qualities and egoism is disappeared.

In this state breathe ceases to exist and suspended automatically. One can reach to this state with tranquil breath only. This is also achieved by Udana Prana technique. A man with haphazard and disturb breath cannot reach even the vicinity of the higher consciousness.

There are more than 70 techniques to control the breath that can calm down mind, body and conscious to make a common human being a spiritual. The spirituality in a life of a man is a purpose less purpose or in other words it is the highest purpose of life. This is governed by breath only.

4.0 To make progress in the spirituality, the basic requirement is the mental peace. For this spiritual aspirant must maintain the tranquil breath i.e. the breath must come and go from both the nostrils simultaneously. If this is maintained, one will feel relax and he will not be perturbed by fear and anxiety.

Tranquil breath must be stable. It gives strength and increases Udana Prana in the human system that is the pre-requisite for the progress in spirituality. With tranquil breath, Prana/life force ascends through Brahmnadi very easily with less effort.

Most of the time for horizontal activity, breath transacts only through senses of actions. However, by tranquil breath blissful stage comes naturally without efforts. This leads to generate 10 types of Nada in the system that makes the human body much healthier as compared to body that has disturbed and haphazard breath.

Initially some efforts are needed to establish the tranquil breath; but later on flow of tranquil breath becomes natural through the human system. Tranquil breath negates the divisible bio-lateral consciousness. It gives one pointed consciousness and concentration.

Furthermore tranquil breath is a divine graceful breath. This gives silence to the mind and increase spiritual power, which is helpful in mergence with supernal. Moreover, silence fulfills the system with harmony. This gives holy bath, removes heterogeneous polarity of mind and helps to be one with the universe.

Even in crisis, it gives peace and negates all selfish motives. It may give Sidhis to the Sadhaka, and all selfish-motives in him cease to exist. No subjective attitude remains in a Sadhaka, he is always full of universal love and brotherhood.

Sadhaka/spiritual aspirant finally leads to spiritual heights of skyness for mergence. One forgets that there is even cosmic consciousness; since he becomes one with the cosmos. With higher spiritual conscious of Sadhaka, nothing can happen wrong on horizontal plane even if he loses awareness on the horizontal plane in the mundane activities.

In higher plane of super consciousness even if he gets momentary awareness with discontinuity of non-awareness, still he becomes/remains blissful with the grace of Almighty. Non-consciousness with discontinuity is bliss of Maya/illusion; it is itself a partial divine state.

Having forgotten awareness at the highest plane of super consciousness even for a few moments, he becomes SAKSHI CHAITNAYA from the state of Kutaksha Chaitanaya that leads him finally to Para Chaitanaya/super conscious/ manifested consciousness.

He is then in absolute silence; and the bliss he experiences in that stateless state is incomparable with any gain in the world. Similar experiences Sadhaka gains with the AUM technique and other evolved techniques.

In AUM technique, while recitation of AUM, M is prolonged longer than A and U. This takes the aspirant to the state of breath suspension and then automatic dissolution/disappearance of breath. This state leads him to transcend time and space, and finally lead to mergence with Absolute with discontinuity.

So, in short any technique followed properly whether Udana Prana technique, AUM technique or Sandhya Gayatri technique, Sadhaka will ultimate experience the stateless state of incomparable bliss; his soul will merge in the Supernal, and he will experience the state of absolute silence being in Savikalpa/ Nirvikalpa Samadhi; it is the state of "Being" beyond time & space; he is in time-less zone.

Finally, he resumes back from this stage with manifested consciousness without egoism but with supreme subtle divine qualities, which prolongs his life with health and happiness along with immense wisdom. All this is achieved by the grace of breath; it is the mean to transcendence of time and space, and to be in the state of well-being.

25

Breathe—Mystery of Relaxation

For success to take step in to the arena of "Being", deep concentration/ awareness is required; it is absolute necessity to control breath; and thought process need to be checked. Thoughtless state must be achieved and mental activities should be dissolved. For this Udana Prana i.e. life force and spiritual energy is required, which can be cultivated/increased/manifested by Kriya yoga, Pranayama and breathing exercises.

All these finally lead to raise the Kundalini power through Sushumna Nadi that helps the Sadhaka for meditation and mergence with the Supernal. However, various relaxation techniques help to give rest to the human system, mind, and nervous system.

These relaxation techniques release the excessive stored energy to the system, which takes the system to slumbering state; they take body and mind to well-being state; but any way these do not increase the Prana Shakti, life force and Udana Prana in the system, which helps to awaken the Kundalini power for transcendence of "time & space" for manifestation of consciousness.

Relaxation as the primary exercise is very useful for smoothening and organizing the breath pattern that is helpful in yoga to restore the mental and physical well being of the human system. Moreover, breath is conceit as the part of Maya/illusion.

And, total relaxation without the help of the breath is not possible; and it is not feasible even to an Avadhoota. Hence breath has immense importance in Yoga, relaxation, survival and mergence.

Furthermore, question does not arise for the ascendance of Prana just by relaxation. However, it is helpful for body, mind and senses to be in relative composed state, and without any conflicting energy to disturb them. So, breath has to be properly channelized for relaxation; but relaxation can not manifest life force needed for spiritual evolution.

In the spiritual path of evolution there are five basic transit locations; namely: Akara; Yakara; Arthchandra; Arohi; and Bindu, which give/transmit various virtues to Jeeva. These are: Rupa; Nama; Bhakti; Priyam; and Asti; respectively.

These physical astral virtues and their representations are the effect of the cause of ascendance in the path of the unknown; particularly Rupa/figure and Nama are beyond Maya/illusion as the divine beauty. By simple relaxation one cannot achieve these virtues; and even the glimpse of these priceless decors in the human life.

Furthermore, it may be noted that Eshwara, Gayatri and Brahma has five faces. They are known as Panch/five Brahmas. Lord Shiva removed one of the head of Brahma because of his false egoism and un-mirthful claim.

Although Brahma is the creator; still there are no temples (a very few) for the worship of Brahma on this earth. Only Vishnu and Shiva are mostly worshipped being the God of Satto Gunna and Tammo Gunna, respectively; and have maximum temples for their worship.

Brahma, the creator, the God of Rajo Gunna is hardly worshipped. This shows that Lord/ Eshwara honors virtues than the potential ability of creation etc. So, being relaxed one can be creative but virtues can only be cultivated by life force and mergence with the "Being".

King and Grahastha/family men are never relaxed because of various responsibilities; namely: the activities of kingdom; and their families, respectively. Their time is not theirs. They hardly spare time to be with the Self and relaxed.

On the contrary, a monk is relatively more relaxed most of time, and not even much bothered for his future. If he gets something, he is happy and even if he does not get, he feels relaxed.

Monk is totally surrendered to the God for his welfare. His time is for his own; he prays, sings the song praising God and feels totally relaxed within himself; and is unaware of his surroundings and comforts. A real monk mostly and truly is in ecstasy.

If such a high order of non-awareness and relaxation prevails to the Sadhaka/spiritual aspirant then he does not need yoga practices for pursuing meditation. Being relaxed, then he is in meditation and with the Almighty.

In short, high level of mental and physical relaxation and unawareness is a stage of Samadhi. Under these conditions, spiritual aspirant does not need practices of yoga.

By deeper relaxation in unawareness, detachment, and without any prejudices, he is in above that of Turiya/ transcendental state; he is totally merged in the devotional songs of his lord without any formal yoga practices. Otherwise mergence with the Supernal with just temporary relaxation is a hypothesis; and it may be true hypothetically and not other wise with a practical viewpoint.

In present modern life living under stresses, full relaxation and unawareness stage is not practicable; one needs breath control, use life force techniques, devotion along with relaxation to the maximum possible extent to be successful in the path of mergence; self realization and to be with the "Being"; and transcendence of "time & space" to manifest his consciousness.

In short, breathe control and to be with the breath is very significant in every walk of life to handle stresses, to get calmness of mind, and to be healthy and happy.

26

Essential Knowledge for Health, Happiness and Well-Being

The gist of basic knowledge is given for health, happiness and well-being; this must be applied for enhancement of longevity of life:

Fatigues is in the first place a reduction of strength by too much digestion work, secondly a clogging up of the heated and consequently narrow-down the blood vessels and thirdly a self empoisoning through the excretion of mucus during the motion.

******

One must chew food of each bite thoroughly because strong secretion of saliva in slow chewing decreases the formation of mucus and helps to prevent overeating. Fruit diet is very helpful, can create positive vibration and take easily near to divinity.

******

Lime is the main mineral for human physical built up, like bones, teethes etc. and is available in fruits and vegetables in plenty. It is said that future generation may be of teeth less due to lack of adequate quantity of lime.

******

Man in perfect health should exhale fragrance. Hair also exhales fragrance and gases depending on body state. Exhale of sulphar di-oxide is the cause of baldness.

******

Disgust, excitement, fear, anxiety, anger, fatigue, pain, injury will stop the movement of digestive track.

******

Fatigue dried up all the digestive secretions and so sometimes foul smell of undigested food appear in the stool.

******

If the food is not properly assimilated and natural function of body do not work properly, then that becomes the root of all evils.

******

Cause of disease is basically because of biologically wrong unnatural food and by each ounce of over nourishment only.

******

When much more waste is in circulation, one feels weak and experiences the bad dreams. Some time fruit juices may cause releasing the poison in the system too rapidly, which might cause high degree of un-easy-ness.

******

If we overstrain the body's life force either through exaggerated sexuality or through excessive mental work then the body is exhausted and falls into a negative condition. Its resistance becomes very low. This creates number of stomach and intestinal disorders. Worry causes in general intestinal disorder. Disappointment and dissatisfaction cause an acid stomach.

******

High temperature is basically effect of positive currents in the body. This destroys the bacilli, which is accumulated during the negative conditions and slowly balanced is maintained.

******

Thyroid glands in the throat keep the body healthy. Ductless glands like thyroid, pineal, pituitary, suprarenal and sexual glands are centers of consciousness. They are chakras and keep the connection between body and mind.

******

Positive pole is located in the head where as negative pole is in the coccyx, the lowest vertebra. Between these poles there is a current of extremely high frequency and short wavelength. Frequent flow of this current make the body healthy and give high degree of mental peace.

******

The perfecting of oneself is the fundamental base of progress and all moral development. There is no surer way to knowledge; nor a better way to help the world than perfecting one's self; nor is there any nobler work or higher science than that of self-perfection. He, who aims at the possession of a calm, wise and seeing/observing mind, engages in the most sublime task.

******

Seed, tree, blossom and fruit are the four-fold order of the universe. Similarly thoughts blossom the deeds, deeds bears fruitage of character and destiny.

******

Way of enlightenment and bliss is to guard him against thinking of unrighteous thoughts.

******

The outer is molded and unified by the inner, and never the inner by the outer.

******

Practice and acquisition of virtue is complete to gain knowledge of truth, and still to know higher secret of life. As man succeeds in acquiring virtues, his mental vibration unfolds it self in knowledge of truth, and it is a knowledge in which he can surely rest and make progress.

******

Path of virtue is the path of knowledge that includes: discipline of physical body; discipline of speech i.e. to avoid gossip and fault finding speech; discipline of inclination i.e. unselfish duty and unlimited forgiveness. And all virtues are abandoned when modesty, gravity and dignity are eliminated from speech and behavior. Neglecting one's duties is nothing less than neglecting virtues.

******

Silence has more influence and enduring power than that noise has in entire humanity. Silence of mind conquers the world by peace and gentleness.

******

A noble and God like character is not a thing of favor or chance, but is the natural result of continued effort in right thinking, the effect of long cherished association with God like thoughts.

******

Outer conditions of a person's life will always be found to be harmoniously related to his inner state. Outer circumstances shape itself according to inner one. Good thoughts bear good fruits and bad thoughts bad fruits.

******

Men do not attract that which they want, but that which they are. Also, men wish and prayers are only gratified and answered when they had harmonized with their thoughts and actions.

******

Suffering is always the effect of wrong thoughts in some direction. It is an indication that the individual is out of harmony with himself, and with law of his being.

******

A man is not rightly conditioned until he is a happy, healthy and prosperous being and these are results of harmonious adjustments of inner with the outer surroundings.

******

Body is a servant of mind. Diseases and health are broadly rooted in thoughts. Sickly thoughts will express themselves through sickly body.

******

Anxiety demoralizes the whole body and lays its door open to the entrance of diseases, while impure thoughts even if one is not physically indulged will soon shatter the nervous system.

******

Change of diet will not help a man who will not change his thoughts. When a man makes his thoughts pure, he no longer desires impure food.

******

Those who don't have central purpose in their life, fall an easy prey to petty worries, fear, trouble etc. To follow royal road of self -control and true concentration in life are the sole purpose of life.

******

A man can rise but still can fall any moment by allowing arrogant, selfish, corrupt, selfish and wrong thoughts to take possession of him. Victory can only be maintained by careful watchfulness otherwise there is certainly a rapid down fall.

******

Self-control is strength, right thought is mastery, and calmness/ silence of mind is the power.

******

Thought is generated from energy/intelligence. And source of thought is the centre of creative intelligence. Also, development of science of creative intelligence is a natural process.

******

Not the desires but un-fulfillment of desires gives the dissatisfaction.

******

Slow breathing gives less oxygen to body, gives rise to less blood lactate, better health control, less B.P., and all that is good memory. All this is achieved by settling down the mental activities.

******

Mind has unique capability. It goes automatically to the position of greater happiness to him. It is not by concentration or by contemplation or by other means. It finds its own direction even by undirected way.

******

Concentration/contemplation is a horizontal superficial way where as Trans-dental meditation or super-consciousness is a vertical cut of deep mental activity. It goes not only by the level of meaning of word but by sound that is life supporting and not life damaging. This makes the mind stand still by spontaneous manner and get full potential of mind.

******

Energy lies in atoms and not in molecules and still in electrons. So if more refined and depth in thought concentration, it will have higher level of energy.

******

In case of acidity in the stomach, milk is not digested. It should either be sucked or sipped by degrees then only it is easily digestable. So Jews don't gulp milk in haste. It becomes even harder to digest when taken with flesh.

******

It is wonderful to imagine that in wealth there is the fear of poverty; in knowledge there is the fear of ignorance; in beauty the fear of age; in fame the fear of backbiters; in success the fear of jealousy; even in the body there is the fear of death.

******

It is well with him who follows the good. On the other hand he loses the goal, which chooses the pleasant. Also, he who is always of restrained mind has right understanding; his senses are controlled like the good horses of a charioteer.

******

From attachment comes longing, and from longing anger grows. From anger comes delusion, loss of memory, which results in ruin of discrimination.

******

Do not do what you want instead do what you like the most.

******

One arrives at the perfect state when mind, body and speech are in proper co-ordination.

******

Forgiveness is holiness. By forgiveness the universe is held together. It is the might of the mighty. Forgiveness is the sacrifice, it is quite of mind. Forgiveness and gentleness are the qualities of self. They represent the internal virtues. Furthermore, harmlessness, truthfulness, non-stealing, purity of body and mind, control of sense organs—are the path of virtues for all.

******

Yoga is the process of stopping the mind stuff. When it is achieved and we are in silence then we shall experience ourselves what we are in reality—the uncreated/un-manifested, the one that creates, manifest itself.

******

If there is God, you will experience and have it by being good. If there is no God, being good is good by it self. So, if man's actions are good, he must be higher being and vice versa.

******

To listen the voice of true self with-in is the blissful state. Then only one becomes infinite—the universal.

******

Knowledge exists, man only discovers it.

******

The higher the moral nature, the higher will be the perception and stronger the will.

******

Those who have attained to the highest spiritual realization, will eventually come face to face with the infinite, and attain to that peace and happiness, which have been attained by all saviors of the world.

******

Faith is not a mental belief in outward facts, but an intuition of the inner being about spiritual things.

******

As per Socrates words "As for me, all I know is that I know nothing".

******

Good manners without sincerity are like a beautiful dead body.

******

Glorious realization is the acquirement of a right understanding of nature of evil.

******

Evil is a self-created shadow. All your pains, sorrows and misfortunes have come to you by a process of undeviating and absolutely perfect law because you deserve and require them. And that first enduring and then understanding them may make you made stronger, wise and nobler.

******

There is no progress apart from enfoldment within.

******

Where there are difficulties to cope with unsatisfactory conditions to overcome, the virtue must flourish and manifest its glory.

******

Turn the disadvantages and miseries of life to account by utilizing them for gaining of mental and spiritual strength.

******

True wealth is the stock of virtues. Making yourself pure and lovable will make you loved by all.

******

To mentally deny evils are not sufficient, it must be by daily practice, be risen above and understood.

******

By daily exercise of silent faith, the thought forces are gathered together, and by daily their strengthening for silent purpose, these forces are directed towards the object of accomplishment.

******

The hour of calmness is the hour of illumination of mind and correct judgment.

******

Where there is sterling faith and uncompromising purity, there is health, success and power.

******

With anger, worry, jealousy, greed or any other unharmonious state of mind, one cannot expect perfect health. True health and true success go together.

******

The foolish wish and grumble, the wise work and wait.

******

The double minded man is unstable in all his ways.

******

Happiness is obtained by gratification (satisfaction) of desire. But later this will cause misery.

******

So long as you search for your own happiness only, you will be sowing the seeds of wretchedness and if you use yourself for the service of others, you will reap a harvest of bliss.

******

Happiness, spirituality and harmony are synonymous. By inward sacrifice, one climbs the ladder of happiness.

******

It is more blessed to give than receive but it must be from heart without any tint of self.

******

Integrity, generosity and love is coupled with energy always bring true prosperous state.

******

Guard yourself against competition if you want high way of righteousness.

******

Meditation is a process of searching uncompromising thought, which allows nothing to remain; i.e. absolute silence that is simple and naked truth.

******

By power of deep meditation every error, every selfish desire, every human weakness is overcome.

******

Truth is that meek and lowly one whose weapons are gentleness, patience, purity, sacrifice, humility, love, and instruments of light. Truth brings inward harmony, perfect justice, and the internal love.

******

Man of truth takes swords against himself only and not against others.

******

It is easy in the world to live after the world's opinion, it is easy in solitude to live after own opinion but the greatest man is he who in the midst of the world keeps with perfect sweetness and independence of solitude.

******

27

To Be in Present Through Breathing

Most of us live in past and think of future although being in present. Hardly any body lives in present. One's mind in general revolves around past incidences or he contemplates about the future.

The present moment slips out from his thinking without fetching him any happiness since he is not with the present moment while being in this moment. Then how can he get happiness when he is not involved in this moment; he is not in present being in present since every thing happens in present.

One must know that past is only in memory and future is unpredictable. One has only the present; he must not lose it; as he loses it, it becomes past; it goes to memory without giving him any benefit.

One must live in present; to concentrate on it; to get fully involved with present with every breath then only he can be immensely happy and contended.

In fact to live in present is most difficult. To live in present is equivalent to control the wind that is flowing at high speed. This is because of the fact that living in present is exclusively being with mind in full consciousness; it is being with his breathing.

As we know mind is like a wind, it always moves; it is never static; it has enormous energy; to control mind is herculean task; to keep it in present and locate it, focus it, needs purely subjective efforts.

Only when one succeeds in his efforts, mind can stay where self desires; and if it is made to stay in present, one can enjoy the activity he is engaged in.

Being in present means as if he is with the "Being"; it is similar to the situation as if mind is concentrated instantaneously; one remains in consciousness/awareness; then only energy is poured in human system.

As this energy is poured in, mind's capacity increases; mind turns from small to great to big to supreme mind; and it follows self; only then one is able to stay in present effortlessly and enjoys present; thus mind ceases to jump gradually to past and future ; mind preserves its energy that can be utilized in any creative efforts.

Even if mind is in present, it swings like the pendulum. It cannot be static; it cannot exist when it becomes static like the clock when its pendulum does not swing. Virtually mind becomes dead in static mode; it is annihilated completely when it is static; in this state breath is suspended; mind is concentrated.

In this condition, it is in silent zone without any thought then it draws energy from Cosmos; it is with the "Being"; it is beyond time & space; this condition leads to manifest consciousness.

However, even being in present, mind is always active; it is energetic. The whole purpose is without making it static being in present; the present is to be explored; and present is to be enjoyed and to be made creative and useful. And this is possible by the concentration/awareness of mind in consciousness in present; this is possible by having full control i.e. awareness on breathing.

The above is possible to use the dynamic energy of the mind being in present to get engrossed in the ongoing activity consciously; and being conscious in the process one is engaged in.

In daily routine work of eating, walking etc, mind must be engrossed fully in the activity; for example in eating process, mind must witness each bite and enjoy the taste of food consciously while chewing. In this way mind without wandering here and there being in present shall enjoy the taste of food consciously.

Still while chewing, it will wander in the present horizontal plane or will wander in the past or future; by self conscious effort it has to put back on the activity, it is engaged in. At least with some discontinuity the mind can be kept on the process of the present on going activity. Only with practice, mind will learn to be in present and will be engrossed with the ongoing activity.

A strong vigilance will be needed by the self consciousness to train the mind, and then only present moment can be enjoyed. Thus, to enjoy every moment, manifested consciousness is needed to have complete vigilance on mind otherwise it will not stay with activity and enjoyment of activity will be lost.

Thus, the activity will be done as a mechanical process without the participation of mind. For example without the presence of mind in the activity of eating one takes food molecules and mixes them with body molecules; he does not enjoy taste of food unless his mind is not engaged in this process.

If the mind is interested in the activity then mind will not roam here and there; it will be engrossed; it will not feel the time; time will be transcendent and one goes beyond time and space; and thus divine energy will be cultivated and one will not be tired of the present activity, he is engaged in.

But, if the activity is not of interest then it will be difficult to keep the presence of mind in the activity; mental energy will be dissipated by roaming of the mind in haphazard direction, and the mind will be tired in no time exhausting all its energy.

In general mind can be concentrated easily by observing the breathing process; by witnessing the breath in and breathe out. In other words, it is more important to witness the on/off process of breathe in and out.

This process will preserve mental energy and mind will cease to roam. With this breathing process slows down; mind also slows down since it takes energy from breath. Thus it will help to keep the mind in present.

Gradually, if this process is continued, subject and object will get merged; breathe is ceased; one reaches to the stage of "Being";

to be beyond "time & space". Thus to be in present, one can draw immense energy from the universe and one can be self realized in due course being in present.

Thus mind will be merged in self and self will be immerged in Supernal with discontinuities; it will transcend time and space. Thus being in present can fetch highest benefit to an individual.

In the nutshell, being in present, one can draw immense satisfaction, preserve energies; one can be in peace; and he can enjoy the activity, he is engaged in; he gets booming energy; he will be relatively mentally and physically fresh; and he will be able to know the self in due course.

In short living in present is living in" Being". Only present is in our control; we must make best use of it being conscious, and be with the breathing as and when required. The change of present to past, and future to present is continuous unending process till we exist.

We can make present futile only being conscious; manifestation of consciousness pours creative divine energy to manifest the happiness of present moment.

We must consciously live in present. This will indeed enhance happiness, well-being and longevity of life. Furthermore, no misdeed will be done by us when we are mentally conscious and live in the manifested consciousness.

28

Silence & Deep Mystic Thoughts

The following quotes on silence and deep mystic thoughts are for the subtle contemplation:

None but right acts can follow right thoughts, none but a right life can follow right acts, and by living a right life all blessedness is achieved.

******

Calmness and patience can become habitual by first grasping through effort calm and patient thoughts, and then continuously thinking and living in them, until these tend to Become second nature; and thus anger and vices pass away forever.

******

Every soul attracts of its own, and nothing can possibly come to it that does not belong to it. To realize this is to recognize the universality of divine law.

******

To mentally deny evil is not sufficient, it must by daily practices, be risen above and understood.

******

Think good thoughts and they will quickly become actualized in your outward life in the form of good conditions.

******

He, who has conquered doubt and fear, has conquered failure.

******

The true silence is not merely a silent tongue, it is a silent mind.

******

Man's true place in cosmos is that of a king and not of a slave; a commander is under the law of good, and not a helpless tool in the region of evil.

******

Taking the first step with good thought, the second with good word, and third with good deed, will open the gate way to paradise.

******

If you think ceaselessly, think upon that which is pure and unselfish, you will surely become unselfish and pure.

******

Shiva joins Shakti or Shakti joins Shiva, no body knows. But, if one can catch hold of Shakti, he has Shiva also.

******

The sun is called the destroyer of darkness, but how and when did sun perceive any darkness? Day and night are the same for the sun; for the sun there is no night; for pure water, there is no salt; one, who is awake, there is no sleep; in presence of fire, Camphor cannot remain. Finally, when He is seen, both worshipper and object of worship vanish.

******

Self is absolute silence. The attempt to describe the self is like trying to express silence with a Brass-Band.

******

Any type of knowledge is bondage for the self-realization. Intellectual knowledge is a relative knowledge. It is just the basic preparation for self-realization. For absolute knowledge, the aid of some other kind of knowledge is needed i.e. the knowledge to know it self. All other will be nothing but just ignorance.

******

It is mystic to know that if the extinguisher of a light is extinguished along with light, then who knows that there was no light; if a person ceased to be during the period of sleep, then who would know that he was in sound sleep; in life to know nothing, one has to become nothing; if dark person stands in darkness, no body can perceive; still he certainly exists and is aware of his existence.

******

If one can see his face without mirror, it means he understands the reality.

******

When even experience dissolves then what is the use of words; in the mirror of words, what is invisible, may be seen; words can liberate self but cannot live with the self; a shadow does not exist where it does not fall, but it also does not exist where it falls; ignorance is, by its very nature is non-existent, then whom should the words destroy; self is the pure knowledge then how the mundane knowledge can know it; the effect of ignorance is ignorance itself; knowledge and ignorance move together; knowledge and ignorance both depend on the word; and when word disappear then nothing remains; every thing is delusion.

******

Self plays happily with himself; the might can imagine every thing except the self; self is self illuminating; there is no other cause for His seeing Himself than Himself; when seer and seen unit then both vanish; whole universe is the luminosity of the self; it is the vibration of the self.

******

Repetition of His divine name with consciousness getting merge in it, is itself a meditation; truly He Himself is every thing; He is the cause of every thing; His name is saver in miseries; no yoga needed if one is merged in His name; when perceiver and perceived are one or become one then mind is redundant/not required.

******

29

Breath and Quantum Jump

Quantum mechanics provides a mathematical description of much of the dual *particle-like* and *wave-like* behavior and interactions of energy and matter. In the context of quantum mechanics, the wave–particle duality of energy and matter, and the uncertainty principle provide a unified view of the behavior of photons, electrons, and other atomic-scale objects.

There was a revolution in physics, consisting of the discovery of quantum physics. The message of quantum physics is this:

The world is not made of matter neither is it determined entirely by material causation that it is sometimes called upward causation because it rises upward from the matter – the elementary particles. There also is a source of downward causation in the world. This source consciousness is the ground of all being.

Furthermore, quantum mathematics does not permit to connect the upward causation-based deterministic theory with experimental data; then how do the possibilities of the theory become actualities of experience simply by looking at them? This is the mysterious "observer effect."

Moreover possible movements of elementary particle make up possible movements of atoms; molecules; cells; brain states; and consciousness. Consciousness itself then is a conglomerate of possibilities; it is a wave of possibility. How can this collapse another wave of possibility by looking or interacting with it? If possibility is coupled with possibility, one gets is a bigger possibility but not the actuality.

For the materialist epiphenomenal model of consciousness, how looking can change possibility into actuality is a logical paradox. It stays a paradox until one recognizes first, that quantum possibilities are possibilities of consciousness itself, which is the ground of all being. And second, that our looking is tantamount to choosing from among the quantum possibilities the one unique facet that becomes our experienced actuality.

The solution of the paradox as discovered is: consciousness is one, non local (not connected with signals) and cosmic, behind the existence of local individuality of two persons. They both can choose from this non ordinary state of one consciousness, which is termed as quantum self. However, it is considered that there is no local individuality or selfishness.

A key point is that quantum downward causation of choice is discontinuous; if it were continuous, a mathematical model could have been framed for this; and the choice would have been predictable; it would then not be free choice.

However, in ordinary state of consciousness of human being, there is no discontinuity. To be aware that we choose is to wake up to the non-ordinary oneness taking a discontinuous leap; it is called a quantum leap/jump.

So, the new paradigm of reality based on the rediscovery of consciousness within science is not only giving us back our free will, but also is identifying the source of that free will as the spirit within us, the oneness that spiritual and healing traditions have always propounded.

The new paradigm is showing us great promise for integrating science and spirit. It is also promising a breakthrough integral approach to medicine that integrates conventional and alternative medicine.

Further more, the field of hypnosis, mediation, telepathy, Reiki, alpha mind-control; yoga is experimenting different ways to study the mind and to bring the mind to perfect control and to aid one to undergo self realization experience.

Quantum jumping is one of the visualization methods, where one will be able to connect to different versions of oneself and enter into a different world; he may step in infinite universe.

The prerequisites needed for quantum jumping are an open mind and the quest to learn more. Basically, there are two ways; one through involving the mind; utilizing full potential of mind. The second way is path of spirit; the path is to annihilate the mind; manifest the consciousness to the maximum possible extent through transcendence of "time & space".

In the first way, each one can use their own mind power, which is still remaining untapped. As the name "Quantum jumping" suggests, one actually jumps in his mind to different universe and different dimensions, parallel to his life and learns more on thinking creatively, gets more knowledge and skills and it also provides more inspiration.

However, through second path, one can draw impression from the inner self, by knowing their other alternate worlds and then transcendence of "time & space" with discontinuities through Quantum Jump; annihilate the mind; to be in timeless zone; being in conscious-less state by quantum jump from conscious state with discontinuities; and return back from this state with manifested consciousness state through automatic quantum jump.

This will enhance divine qualities, wisdom, Well-being and prolong life with health and happiness. This is the highest superior quantum jump and it is a step into "Being"; and return back to the awakening consciousness.

According to the quantum theory, the physical world is just a mirage. The quantum jumping may be called the "human thought transference" process. It is through the art of concentration, meditation and transcendence.

This transforms a human being and in hence the virtues and subtle qualities. This is possible only through breathe control and without breathe control quantum jump is not viable.

Many people have increased the capacity of the brain power and have trained their mind to open their creative ideas and to solve difficult situation easily. This has helped them to achieve better in both the personal lives as well as in the career front. By doing the quantum jumping, one is able to link himself to the subconscious mind. This connection will help in solving issues better as they will be able to take quicker and correct decisions even in crucial circumstances and they start believing their intuitions.

Many people who have bad habits like smoking, drinking alcohol, indulging in wrong perception of life have now developed a lot of self control and have quit their bad habits. Quantum jumping will help in creating more positive feelings and to nullify the negative thoughts.

The mindset is improved and the people who practice quantum jumping are able to spend wisely and save better, than when compared to their earlier status. Those who start quantum jumping develop a special interest to learn some new skills and a few could find the real purpose of life.

In addition, the theory is that there are many parallel universes, as many as one would care to imagine, possibly an infinite number and within each universe. If one would like to merge in universe around him self, he has to take quantum jump since whole universe is one single identity; difference lies in manifestation of consciousness.

Universe has infinite consciousness as against finite consciousness of an individual; merging with universe, taking a quantum leap/jump in to the universe, certainly manifests his consciousness with multifold subtle virtues.

One needs to get himself into that relaxed creative state that is associated with the practice of meditation. This can be done using binaural beats or more traditional methods such as calming the mind, concentrating on breathing, thinking of nothing; taking the quantum jump by suspending breathe; thus transcending time and space and then take step into "Being".

Thus, by quantum jumping one can be self realized; one can enhance longevity of life, wisdom, well-being; health and happiness. In short, quantum jump is not possible without having full command on breathing.

30
Consciousness and Conscious Breathing

Health, happiness, well being & Life extension through breathing and manifestation of consciousness; step into being; to be beyond time & space; requires in depth understanding of consciousness/awareness and conscious breathing since we all are the part of all prevailing, omnipresent, omniscient existence and infinite consciousness, which is present everywhere even in each smallest possible being.

However, it cannot be easily perceived since light cannot be perceived in overall spread light. Light it self is merged in the light around us; light in light cannot be distinguished; and nor sun rays can be differentiated from sun light; they are the same and are not different from the sun shine. So, our consciousness is a part and parcel of universal consciousness; we all are part of the universal being.

This is not possible to perceive by a human being unless and until he gets totally merged; and becomes part of universal consciousness consciously; as well as becomes one of the "Being". On the contrary, one needs to stretch the canopy of his consciousness to the infinite level to completely perceive overall universal consciousness, which is also not possible for a human being.

It is all considered as philosophical complexity; and in general it is not understood mentally and not even spiritually at the core depth of it. This is the dilemma of consciousness. However, one can understand conscious breathing; it can be practiced by self efforts and immense benefits can be acquired to enhance the subtle qualities.

This universe is like a vast ocean. Billions of waves existing in an ocean are basically part of the ocean. It is well understood that ocean can exist without waves, but waves cannot exist without ocean. Waves are the part of the ocean, but ocean is not the waves alone. Similarly, we are the part of the universe, we exist in it. However, universe can exist without us, but not we without it.

As waves and ocean both are integrated, part of the ocean is in the waves, and waves are in the ocean. Ocean can sustain itself without waves, but not the vice versa.

In the same way all living being sustained in this universe, but the universe can be without the living beings. Likewise living being is a part of universal being, but universal being is not merely the living being. Universal being exists without living being, but not a living being can exist without the grace/ light of the universal being.

Waves are generated in the ocean by various disturbances in the ocean, and go above the normal levels of the ocean with the vigorous energy, and when the energy is exhausted, waves fall / come back to the normal level and merge with the ocean. After mergence there's no difference that can differentiate ocean water with that of the waves.

This play of the waves is continued on the surface of the ocean when the waves rise, it can be identified even from the distance, but when waves merge they loose their identity. Waves have no identity in the ocean, and without the ocean.

The appearance of a wave and its disappearance and re-appearance in the ocean is the ocean phenomenon. Similarly, birth of a living being and his mergence in the universal being is the phenomenon of universal being.

In the limited time span, wave is born, becomes violent, shows its youth, tries to go higher and higher from the sea level, and finally loses its energy, and instantaneously falls down, and merges with the ocean, and disappears in the ocean without having its identity. And, thus the life cycle of both high and low tides are completed as if both are one, similar and identical to each other, as they appear a few moments before.

This unending cycle goes on in the ocean similar to the birth and death of a living being on this earth, and in this universe. From this, it is worth perceiving that our existence on this planet is just temporary and nothing is permanent.

The basic question then arises why to cultivate much possession during this short existence, and spend complete life span and energy on such cultivations and possessions?

It is very evident from this inference that one needs to have deeper philosophical insight to see the life very closely to know its temporary existence, and to do some valuable cultivations and contributions to get more wisdom of this omnipresent nature and consciousness in a short span of human life; step into "Being" and to be beyond time & space.

It should be all the more clear that one has to merge back from where he was originated i.e. in universal; which is beyond time & space.

Furthermore, if the wave is light and energetic then only it can go higher above the ocean surface, and visualize the beauty of ocean. Similarly, a person who is less materialistic, and lives merely by needs and requirements for proper survival, can be more energetic, intrinsic and spiritual, and can travel the vertical journey of life more comfortably with detachment.

This can help him to merge in the beauty of the Self and witness the beauty of universal "Being"; and thus he can become the man of real wisdom with enlightenment and self realization; then he can easily transcend time and space with consciousness, without the traces of ignorance.

On the contrary, the vertical height gained in the spiritual science by the highly materialistic person will be very limited; he will be mostly wondering in his possessions and material collections; he will be in outer most periphery of the divinity, far away from the real wisdom of life; and to be beyond time and space will be nightmare for him.

In a nutshell, from the above analysis, scientifically it can be co-related that what so ever is transpiring macroscopically in the ocean, the same is happening microscopically to the tiny waves and each drop of ocean water.

The nature of the wave, its quality, its energy level, its turmoil or quietness indicates the real intrinsic happening at the bottom of the ocean. Turmoil on the surface of the sea is clear picture of disturbances due to various unknown reasons in the heart of the ocean.

Similarly, if a person is aware of his true nature and mental turmoil from time to time in his manifested consciousness, and all the positive and negative conflicts within himself, then he will not be far away macroscopically of all the disturbances in his surroundings, non-friendly and friendly thoughts of persons, he is dealing with.

Furthermore, he will easily perceive positive and negative attitudes of his near and dear persons around him; and also it will not be difficult for him to know universal and natural happening macroscopically by his self awareness/consciousness and self realization.

Finally, it will depend on how much he has evolved him self in the art of self-awareness and self-consciousness. Breath is the medium of communication between the inner and outer world since the air, we breath go in our system is from the external atmosphere. So, if we are deeply conscious of breathing, we can be conscious of both inner and outer happenings.

Moreover, after knowing and getting aware-of and being conscious of, what must one should do, take action, modulate himself, will depend on his capability and his ability to glimpse into beyond time & space, from where he will get the complete knowledge intuitively.

Some times knowingly or unknowingly good and bad can happen, and these discontinuities might surprise him, and put him on the platform that makes him to realize that there is much less in his control being a human being.

Finally, this will make him to perceive that every thing is in the purview and control of universal "Being". This will be his self-experience by the art of developed consciousness/awareness as a result of self-realization. This makes him to experience power and omnipresence nature of universal "Being", which is beyond time & space; besides fully knowing that he is finite creature in universe and nothing more.

In short, if a person is aware of his inner happenings, his own true nature, and all that is going on in himself, in his consciousness; he will not be far away from the universal happenings macroscopically.

This is because of the fact that universal mind and mind of a person belongs to the same universal consciousness/origin. The difference is that human mind is unaware of; it is sleepy; unconscious; such that it has lost its potential and higher capabilities microscopically but the universal consciousness is fully awaken and all around.

In fact, any turmoil of universe including that in his daily life reflects and creates high frequency low energy levels throbbing in the conscious human mind, which an ordinary undeveloped mind is not aware of. So, by knowing himself, by self-awareness, by self consciousness, by self-realization, and by self-enlightenment; and to be beyond time & space; taking step into "Being"; one can be much better aware of this infinite universe.

However, he cannot be master of the universe since human mind; human consciousness is finite and has finite capabilities; hence he cannot be aware of the universal phenomenon in totality.

But, if within his finite limits, he can modulate, influence and put efforts to change by very close awareness and being conscious of the self and by manifesting his consciousness to be beyond time & space, his capabilities shall be enhanced.

Finally, glimpses of to be beyond time & space shall immersed him in timeless zone, which is the era of universal "Being"; he becomes part of the "Being"; as there remains no difference between he and He as between ocean and drop. Similarly, he will be equipped with same potential and characteristics as that of universal "Being". Thus, by manifestation of his consciousness, he can enhance his well being.

Conscious breathing acts as a reliable tool to achieve this state. Without having conscious command on breathing he cannot transcend time & space; he is unable to enhance health, happiness and well-being.

In general, a common man spends most of his time in unconscious ignorance state; basically he is in inert/Tama sic state. Raja sic person is always active; he is generally conscious and is in awakening state but he is in Maya/illusion like a Tama sic person.

However, divine/Satvik person is look like as if he is in unconscious state like that of Tama sic person but divine person is always in manifested conscious state after transcendence of conscious state to conscious-less state. His conscious-less state is divine; he rolls between divine unconscious and manifested conscious state.

Divine person can maintain this state by conscious breathing. Breath is a master however core consciousness is light/soul. Consciousness has subtle control on the breath; breath is life.

31

To Overcome Boredom Through Breathing

Most of us, some time or another, generally feel boredom. Boredom has become major part of life. We feel bored at home; we feel bored at work; and we feel boredom some time even talking to some one. Staying with some one of different temperament generates more boredom in us. In any walk of life, in any activity, generally people feel boredom after some time.

No activity and no involvement with any person gives prolonged contentment and happiness to some of us. However, mind of many people hardly get time to feel instances without boredom. In general, degree of boredom varies from person to person.

There are very few people in this world who don't feel boredom as if they have never experience what boredom is. It is similar to light which has never experienced darkness.

This is because of the fact that darkness disappears instantaneously as light appears. Light does not know what darkness is. Both cannot be friends and cannot exist together. Darkness cannot experience light since as light appears, darkness vanishes. Darkness and light cannot co-exist together; either there is darkness or light.

Light experiences that it has never come across darkness; darkness blames that light does not allow him to exist in its presence. This is the dilemma. Whom to blame? Both are right in their prospective. In the same way darkness of boredom in life cannot exist in presence of light of physical or mental activities. Darkness of boredom can appear in absence of engagement or occupation of interest and liking.

The question arises, why we feel bore? This has to be deeply analyzed. This is a vast world; no two persons are alike; every body of us is different. Nature has made variety of leaves of the plants. Even leaves of one plant don't match to each other in totality. All leaves are unique by one way or other.

In fact, we have to interact with many people in our day to day life, and every body is different physically, by temperament, by thinking, by way of living, by way of speaking and by many more aspects. In fact every body is unique.

Still we cannot stop interacting with many people in life for our social and professional existence even if we don't like them. Life has to move with variety of patterns and with variety of people around us. If we feel boredom with people, our survival will be at stake. However, we can minimize interaction but it cannot be completely avoided for our existence.

We have to tolerate temperament of many people around us. In the same way, we have varieties and different pattern of energies in us having broad spectrum of frequencies, we have to live with this variety otherwise we cannot exist.

Some times, we like some thing but at another occasion, we don't nourish it. However, nothing has changed; things are same, environment is same but instead our liking, disliking has surfaced. Why? It means some thing got modulated in us with time, or with circumstances or by other reasons, which has affected us.

This cannot be something external; it has come from within us without our knowledge. To perceive, the complete scenario, it shows that we need to analyze our inner thinking; our inner happenings; modulation of our mind; our thoughts; our intrinsic built up and intrinsic energies.

This means main cause of boredom is from inner core of our mind and emotions; it has nothing to do much from the outer world. In this world, there is hardly any significant change that occurs in short span of time. Only subject is changing; objects are the same.

In other words, we are changing. Our inner energies are flowing like river water; by stepping in water and lifting the feet to put the next step in water, the same water will no more be there. Flow of water is changing the water it self, its molecules, and particles in it. However, it looks that there is no change in water in the span of changing the position of our feet.

In fact every thing is changed, which we neither recognize nor perceive. Similarly our mood changes spontaneously like flow of water and this brings boredom some times. The accumulation of many changes in us with time, which effects us, we cannot understand; although there is no significant change externally with environment, surroundings etc.

For example we nourish certain type of food as we take first bite of it; but with time after a few bites same food does not give us that taste, nourishment and liking as compared to the first bite since our hunger goes on diminishing as we eat.

In the same way, as per the law of nature, we start feeling boredom after some time with in us being with same people; in fact, we are changing and this causes boredom as a reaction of change in our attitude because of our inner conditions although people around us remain the same with their attitude and behavior.

As a reaction to our inner feel of boredom, we would like to have change. Change of partners is the major cause of this internal modulation, which is the appearance of boredom in the core of our heart. In fact boredom is a part of universally accepted phenomenon in attitudes and behavior but its impact is variable on each one of us.

In real life, any type of discontinuity in continuity of interaction brings back the original mood and appeared boredom is diluted. Temporary void and discontinuity in terms of time or engagement with different activity is the basis to overcome boredom in day to day living.

This needs to be followed to be happy in all occasions in the realm of continuity of life for significant evolution without getting and feeling boredom.

In other words temporarily change in the on going activity, replenishes our energy; and thus, boredom with the ongoing activity disappears. Meeting different people and changing environments also helps to create discontinuity of boredom of our mind.

A mother is never tired and nor bored with loving her child; she gets divine happiness to be with her child all the time. It is divine food for her. In the same way, our work, our profession, if it is of our utmost liking to us then it will never gives us feeling of tiredness and we will never get bored. Darkness of boredom will never enter in the light of our work of self liking.

Our creative work of self choice will never experience the presence of boredom as light never experiences darkness. In other words, we must engage in activity of our choice; activity should not be dumped on us. Any activity if forced on us against our choice or liking will make us disinterested and create boredom in us within no time.

In the same way, we must be careful assigning activity to our juniors and to our children so that this must be of interest to them. The same is equally valid for us that our all the activities should revolve around our liking and our interest; it will make us healthy, happy and we will never feel tired for long hours of working and darkness of boredom will never enter in our mental territory.

As we know that our spiritual masters, living all alone without any external engagements, have never felt boredom of any kind in their lives; they were always healthy and happy all the time. It means that the best way is to avoid the boredom of any kind is to engage the self with creative activity of self liking; to transcendence of time and space to manifest consciousness; and to be with the Self when ever there is spare time.

This increases mental potential and keeps us above all type of boredom in life; our life becomes purposeful for creative, healthy and useful activities for the self and for the society. To manifest the consciousness has infinite scope.

As we manifest consciousness, we would like to manifest it further; it gives us more and more happiness; it is unending bliss. Under the canopy of manifestation of consciousness, even traces of boredom will never be felt.

Furthermore, we will always be in light of contentment through self engagement and darkness of boredom will never be experienced. So, discontinuity from boredom will be automatically achieved in the realm of continuity of life without any restrains.

If our aim is the achievement of perfection in life then there is no time for us to accommodate boredom; this disappears in void; and no further efforts are required to achieve discontinuity of boredom in life; it gets disappeared for ever.

In addition whenever one feels boredom in life, he must be with his flow of breath; he must be conscious of breath in and breathe out. He must learn art of breathing. Breath must be his master in time of aloneness.

This engages the mind and replenishes the mental energies; this maintains calmness of mind and directs it towards divine light to enhance the subtle qualities of life. Consequently boredom is discontinued to exist in any form in the realm of existence for evolution in life.

Any activity in life creates boredom after some time; but discontinuity of on going activity for some time replenishes the boredom and we are fresh to resume the activity again. Same may happen with the activity, we like the most. However, activity of transcendence of time and space, being with the divinity, never creates any boredom since as one goes in depth of divinity, joy goes on manifesting.

It bestows infinite joy without any limitation; there is no boredom even in vicinity of divinity, and divine mergence in chanting of His name with awareness in silence and being with the Self.

Self is unending joy and much above boredom. Support of breathing technique and being with the discontinuity of breath, one can draw unlimited inner subtle energy to be happy and to transcend any boredom in life. In fact, the boredom will never be felt.

In short, breath should be accepted as master to overcome any boredom any time in life for executing any required activity.

32

Science of Breathing to Overcome Egoism

Egoism is very significant attribute in human personality. Without egoism, no work can be accomplished. Certain level of egoism is required to get going the life. Egoism gives mental force to work, to exert, to achieve the goal. Without egoism there is no desire to achieve any thing and no energy to execute.

Egoism attributes power to work and to accomplish some thing unique. Certain amount of egoism is always required to be active in realm of existence in life.

On the contrary, egoism of an individual does not allow listening even good view points of others. Egoism cannot tolerate peers; egoistic person cannot tolerate competition by another; he cannot tolerate that he is inferior to any one.

Even if egoistic person does not know, he projects as if he knows every thing. He does not honor knowledge of any one; he discards even his superiors. He lives in his own world of thoughts.

Egoistic person always finds faults in others. He considers himself most superior in all respects. He always desires that every one must respect him although he himself does not bother for any one. He is always full of anger; he cannot tolerate defeat in any sphere. He has no regards for virtues of any one.

Egoistic person does not take any responsibility of self defeat and group defeat; he always blames others for loss and defeat; he always tries to manipulate statements and his promises. He is not trust worthy in any walk of life. He does not command intrinsic respect from peers, subordinates, family members, and his own kith and kin's.

Egoistic person is always shrewd and diplomat; he misleads others to show his superiority for his guidance. He always criticizes others if they don't succeed by following the path he recommended even if his recommendation is inferior. He never takes responsibility of any failure in realm of his life.

Broadly speaking a child must have certain egoism to negate his parent's wish and thinking to have self steam to execute what he desires in life. His egoism should not be curbed to build his personality in earlier age till he gains some wisdom. Gradually he must be guided to align on right track and obey his parents.

As child grows, his ego has to be shed down for learning and accumulation of good habits. If one remains in egoism at the learning stage, he cannot get better education; he cannot cultivate wisdom. His egoism must be transformed to manifest mental energy to learn and acquire wisdom. However, certain level of built in egoism helps to be a better student otherwise child will remain dull. But, egoism must be in defined boundaries.

Basically egoism is a tool; it must be sharpened precisely. At different occasions and at various instances it has to be shed down. It must be known that for gaining higher wisdom, egoism is a big hindrance. If one is not able to dissolve and overcome egoism in life, he is likely to be deprived of higher success in life.

No body bothers for an egoistic person. He will not have good friends. Only "yes" men will surround him to boost his egoism and take his egoism to a higher level for their selfish intrinsic motives.

Peers will not be co-operative with an egoistic person; he will be left all alone in realm of continuity in life. In realm of continuity in life, number of discontinuities appears in his life when he feels loneliness and no body shares unhappy moments of his life with him. No one will be sympathetic for his failures.

Lack of wisdom because of his egoism creates void in realm of his existence. Hence egoism is to be applied judicially with discrimination in life. There is no life without egoism and with egoism one has to be extremely cautious.

In realm of life people generally have egoism of power, money, position, knowledge, beauty, and untimely success in life. Some have egoism of capable and successful children, honorable caste and family, and honor in society.

Any cultivated talent makes a man egoistic; he starts considering others very inferior. His egoism is reflected in his gestures, his looks, his talks and even his walk projects egoism. He/she dresses in such a way so that his egoism is reflected to show his unique personality.

In society, egoism is based on comparison; one compares himself with peers and considers him superior and thus he boosts his own egoism. When cycle of life takes a gloomy turn, he looses prestige, power and whole achieved success is drained due to various unforeseen reasons, then such an egoistic person feels miserable. Then no one cares for him.

No body consoles him; he is left all alone; his egoism disappears. If he some how he is able to visualize his inbuilt personality, his past, his egoistic way of living, then only he repents in his life.

The basic question is as to how egoism is to be transformed in positive mental energy for overall materialistic and spiritual growth for honorable living.

It must be known that human being in subtle way revolves around mind, consciousness and spirit.

Egoism is a subtle part of mental energy. It needs to be transformed in creative positive energy. First of all one needs to look within himself; he needs to analyze subtle mental tendencies of his mind; these can be sex, greed, anger, undue attachment besides built in egoism in his personality.

If one perceives that he has egoistic personality then he is required to be vigilant of his mind; he has to be conscious of his activities and his attitudes. All actions, he must perform with full awareness.

If he develops awareness in his all activities, he will conceive as if some one is watching him. In that case no egoism can influence his personality.

As per the law of "observer effect" of quantum mechanics, his all activities will turn to be refined if he is conscious and vigilant for his activities. This will consume his egoistic mental energy; transform him intrinsically; and this way of living will make him calm and change his life style. His egoism will be dissolved gradually.

Furthermore, awareness of breath and being with discontinuity of breath facilitates him to absorb cosmic energy of universe in moments when he is in state of void i.e. when his inner breath comes out/ exits and fresh breath yet to enter the system. This will cultivate subtle virtues in his personality and turn him to be ego-less personality gradually.

Above process gradually transform his egoistic nature and his egoistic pattern of thinking and living. This process can be further enhanced by transcendence of time and space, by annihilation of mind and manifestation of consciousness.

Thus, excessive egoism can be controlled; one can change his attitudes in realm of life; he can become better listener; he can develop nature/habit of having regards for others; his subtle virtues and qualities will be enhanced.

In this way, he will develop liking for others and gradually he will transform himself to a perfect human being with developed intrinsic subtle qualities. His physical well-being will be improved and he will have overall better materialistic development.

Unless the egoism is not transformed, one cannot surrender. Without surrendering wisdom in life will be far away. One can only be on periphery of learning and understanding without shedding intrinsic egoism. He can not reach to the centre. Centre is the source of energy, wisdom and deep knowledge. Centre is a governing force. Only an ego-less man can reach the centre to be wise.

One has to be conscious in all his activities to overcome egoism in life. Developed egoism in realm of life has to be shed down consciously to gain the nectar of divine wisdom, and to be self realized.

In short, he has to be an innocent like child consciously shedding his egoism to enter in the regime of Almighty and to become one with Him. Then only he can complete the journey of human life successfully.

It is not the path of ignorance with egoism but it is the path for a knowledgeable person who has consciously shed his egoism and cultivated childlike innocence in realm of his life. He, then, is a perfect human being.

Science of breathing can assist him to be egoless. He must observe breath in and breathe out; he must develop the art to be with discontinuity of breath. In this way subtle divine energy will pour automatically in his senses, and gradually his built in egoism will be diluted; finally it will be nullified and he will turn out to be a humble person without even traces of egoism.

33

Breath—The Invisible Divine Force/ Energy

Following quotes from dormant human science on breath gives immense knowledge and out standing significance of breath in all walks of our physical, mental and spiritual life:

Breath is Master. It is bundle of closely knitted five elements: earth, water, air, light/fire and sky. Breath is also Gayatri—the protector of body as light and light is energy.

******

Our reaction to the situation is directly proportional to the breath pattern. In depression state of an individual, the breath is always heavy and the waves are wide.

******

By Kriya Yoga technique, breath can be suspended.

******

Before entering into the system, breath is of non-atomic nature. On entering in the system, it splits in to five elements.

******

Cosmos contains more of the sky element. Breath of cosmos emerging out of the self churning of the nameless void is called life force. In Sri vidya, it is called "Viswakundilini". It is breath of all.

******

Cosmic life force is the breath of universe. During interaction of individual breath and cosmic breath, life force flows through Sushumna.

******

Breath is both centre and circumference. The expansion of the centre into a circle of the breath is universe.

******

When vacuumed is created in the system i.e. when there is no breath; it is the state of vacation of breath. Then only the spirit charges the void in the system and divine energy appears.

******

Turiya is vacuumed state i.e. void stateless state during meditation.

******

In this vacuumed state, Udana Prana is generated and corrects the system and makes it healthy. Udana Prana is life force. This creates peace, bliss and joy in the system.

******

Breath can be one's own Guru/master and gives proper direction, when needed.

******

Mind is conquered by life force energy. It is produced by breath; it is the secret of breath.

******

Life force is also Annarasa. One can live on life force without taking solid food.

******

Generally for a common man only one half of breath goes to Annahata i.e. heart centre and remaining half is returned without any function.

******

From void i.e. elemental sky cosmic life force is born. It gives birth to atom to mahat/air to wind to fire to water to earth to vegetable kingdom and then to unicellular organism.

******

Basically void becomes five elements by throbbing and then transforms to Mahabhutas, which descend to every atom of the body; at heart it is air; at manipura it is fire; at swadhistanam it is water; and at mooladhara it is earth.

******

In void they all are woven as Jadha/stable before any transformation. The deep secret of breath is from void to void.

******

It is wonderful to know and practice to take breath from mouth; to store it in naval centre; and then empty it and create total vacuumed. This process of breathing reduces the body heat and makes it cool.

******

If there is pain in the hands, breath must be stored in Vishudhi chakra for some time. In general stored breath is to be moved to location where ever there is pain.

******

In case of bulging out of stomach, sunnayaka/vacuumed of breath through Manipura is to be maintained.

******

For problem in any part of the body, life force is to be created in the body, and then after bringing this life force on the tip of fingers, it should be sent to the effected part, where cure is needed.

******

Breath stored in Muladhara, tackles the problem of kidney and lower organs; at swadhistanam stored breath tackles the digestion problems; at manipura stored breath cures stomach pain issues.

******

If right nostril is blocked then problems of right side of the body are piled up, and if left nostril is jammed/blocked then problems of organs located at left side occur.

******

In general exit of the breath shall be elongated to cure the body from various diseases. Tranquil breath removes miseries of life.

******

Basically one must observe rhythm, elongate breath with equal-distribution of storing and vacating of breath for good health.

******

Listening of reverberations of own breath coupled with divine melody is Inner Nada. It is called Antarnadanu -sandhana.

******

In AUM, A stands for earthiness, U stands for Watery and M for Light. Crescent on Aum is Prana and dot (.) is for Akasa. The sequence for descending order is from infinite to void to sky to Prana to Light to Water to Earth.

******

When breath flows from right nostril, it is termed as vertical breath i.e. from Brahm Nadi. When it flows from left nostril, it is termed as horizontal breath i.e. from Indira Nadi.

******

Breath flowing from both nostrils equally (in and out) is called tranquil breath. It is Ekatara breath that creates vacuumed or void in the system and strengthens it.

******

Taking breath from both the nostrils simultaneously indicates the breakage of triangle of the Karmas. This situation/aspect is like Bindu/point of Sri Chakra where both Shiva and Shakti exist together.

******

Sandhya: when it is manifested, it is beyond Maya/illusion, and when it is un-manifested, it is Lalita. Breath is Maya.

******

Cessation of breath indicates the presence of God. Mind cannot be at one place even in presence of one breath.

******

Creating Vacuumed by taking away the breath renders mind concentration. Even this cannot be adequately achieved by suspension of breath.

******

Silence of mind cannot be achieved in presence of even the mildest breath. Prana and life force must exit from Sahasrara for perfect silence and mind control. Also, breath/Prana must pass through Sushumna Nadi and must merge with light for absolute silence.

******

If the breath is kept or it rests beyond Dahara Chakra, at Ajana or near to the soul, the decay of the body is very slow. If breath is below Dahara Chakra, decay of body is very fast.

******

The movement of breath as Prana to Apana is horizontal breath and vertical movement of Prana and Apana through Sushumana up to Ajna is vertical divine breath.

******

At Ajna breath is called Pratyagatma but at Sahasrara it is termed as Sada Siva. At Unmani Chakra when Pratyagatma loses its cognizance of identity with Supernal than breath has no role to play as light; or as wind; or as other element; like water or earth etc.

******

On vertical journey, breath must merge at every Chakra; so that at Sahasrara it remains as pure light only; and get easily merge with Supernal.

******

34

Effect of Synchronous Breathing for Mutual Cordiality in Realm of Life

Human being with physical body, mind, intellect and consciousness with complex emotional feelings is an integrated and complex interwoven system. Human behavior is never the same; it is variable with time, space and causation.

While interacting with some one, his behavior is variable and mutable; one cannot take it granted that there will be mutual co-cordiality with two persons all the time during their mutual interaction. This we experience every day in our daily life.

Why this happens? What is its cause? This has to be deeply analyzed and understood. This must be understood that this is beyond intrinsic motives. However, this do happens in realm of life but such situations can not be easily grasped during interaction.

But, if it is understood then one can take corrective measures as and when needed. What is being analyzed here is beyond interior motives of two interacting persons; and is closely linked with the human systems, which is a process and is a function of time.

As we know, our system physically is equipped with two nostrils for breathing. We can breathe from both nostrils. But, some time we breathe from left nostril and some time from right nostril. It depends on blockage of passage in nostrils; one of them does not have clear passage and other one have a free passage for flow of air.

Both nostrils are always in operation but some time left is active and another time right is active; this depends on rhythm of the human system, which is closely linked with mind, brain and physical body. Also, depending on rhythm of human system, breathe pattern changes.

Air passage through nostrils changes; and unknowingly nostril through which we were breathing earlier changes to other nostril. The shift takes place from left to right nostril or vice versa; the duration of breathing from any of the nostril depends on status and condition of human system.

After completing circuit from left to right nostril or right to left nostril, passage of air becomes clear from both nostrils; and then one starts breathing from both the nostrils simultaneously without any resistance on the passage. Thus, after completion of this cycle i.e. from left to right nostril or vice versa and then simultaneously from both nostrils. The breathing cycle repeats.

Thus, after some time one of nostril gets blocked automatically and cycle gets repeated by it self as per the condition prevails in human system and the mental status of a human being.

This above system of breathing is continued automatically unless it is disturbed manually by self efforts by forcefully allowing the passage of air through blocked nostril or by the conditions prevailed in the human system.

Furthermore, left nostril of human system is connected to Ida Nadi; it is called moon Nadi. Right nostril is connected to Pingala Nadi; it is called sun Nadi. When one takes breath through moon Nadi, one is mentally active and cool. On the other hand breathing through sun Nadi, makes a human being physically energetic and active. But when breathing is though both Nadis together, it is called tranquil breathe; it is the state when one can effortlessly fall in meditation.

When two people interact during discussions and some activity of mutual interest, it is found that some time they are cordial with each other as if they are in the same frequency; but on another occasion they are not cordial during interaction. This may happen in course of interaction also when all other conditions are unchanged without any arbitration.

If status and conditions are examined, we can find that earlier both were breathing though identical side of nostrils; they were in synchronous breathing so their interaction was smooth; and their frequency matched with identical thought process.

This was later changed because of mismatch of their breathing pattern; synchronous breathing pattern was disturbed. This was because of the fact that one started breathing through different nostril because of change in rhythm of his system, which has disturbed pattern of synchronous breathing prevailed with other person; finally there occurs mismatch in their synchronous existing breathing pattern.

To more closely understand synchronous breathing, one needs to be conscious during close mutual interaction. If one finds the situation is getting beyond control, he must observe synchronicity of his breath pattern; he must immediately change synchronicity of breath pattern by forcefully opening the closed nostril and should start breathing through this earlier closed nostril. Very soon, it will be understood that mutual cordiality is getting established without undue discussions and arguments.

The above is a subjective approach and its authenticity can be proved in day to day life consciously and by manifesting the awareness of synchronicity of breathe pattern.

The same technique can be applied for changing one's own mood and temperament as and when required. Shifting of breathing from left to right nostril or vice versa from right to left nostril by self efforts by opening the closed nostril, helps to transform one's own mood and temperament as the environment demands.

These are very helpful techniques and should be used when it is essential. In general one must try to live as per the rhythm of his system, and he must not disturb the prevailing rhythm of physical and mental systems unless and until it is required.

In short, synchronous breath pattern gives an edge to get involved smoothly with people of different temperaments as and when required; it transforms the personality spontaneously to manage the situation. One needs to have manifested awareness to deal with the synchronous breath pattern.

To manifest the awareness, one needs to manifest consciousness by the process of transcending mind to step in the era of timelessness; to be beyond time and space by temporarily suspending the breathe. Prayer, devotion and blessings of universal oneness are the prerequisites to climb this mysterious ladder.

In fact by self awareness in realm of life, one will definitely experience the impact of breathing and its pattern; he is forced to realize that breath is master.

35

Well-Being, Health, Happiness, Longevity and Transcendence Through Breathing

Well-being, health and happiness is the basic interest of a human being in life; every body wants to live longer; medical science and holistic science revolve around means and ways to extend life, health and happiness of a human being. To enhance the life span and health is being tackled through different directions.

All directions and angles have their own positive prospective and have rendered wonderful results in multiple ways. By good food habits, regular exercise, by proper medical care, by stress free life, and by taking care of many health concerning aspects, one can on an average live for thousand months.

How healthy and trouble free one lives, it varies from person to person. However, one can extend his life further and live healthy and happily provided he clearly understands his physical body, his mental turmoil and his own well being.

Furthermore, if he orients his energies towards subject i.e. physical body besides judicially using the present development of medical sciences for his welfare, he is immensely benefitted.

Subjective human science enriches the subject i.e. one's individual physical body, a tool that need to be supervised, looked after and need to be felt with the subjective knowledge.

All the signals of the body are to be monitored and then corrective actions are to be taken by subjective ways. For this inner vigilance is needed to be developed; one has to be introvert to understand himself and to be with the self.

Moreover, one has to understand the self deeply; and he has to apply the accumulated knowledge of the self since subject is to be taken care of by self means only.

It has to be visualized and perceived that human physical body is closely linked with other four bodies, which are dormant in human system. Gross physical body is closely coordinated with Pranic, Mental, Intellectual and Spirit bodies of human system.

One has to develop himself to feel the other bodies of the system besides having closely monitored his physical body. If one of the bodies is not properly nourished, it will affect the remaining four since all are closely interwoven.

These five bodies govern our thoughts, words and actions. There is such a complex feed back system among all these bodies that each body affects another body very closely.

Among them spirit is the finest, and physical body is gross. Pranic, mental and intellect bodies are the "Karan Sharir" and may be called subtle bodies. Until complete cohesiveness is not attained in all these bodies, blissful state, the finest state cannot be perceived.

Only by achievement of cohesive state and blissful state, the well being of all the bodies are assured; and then only the extension of life, heath, happiness with complete well-being can be achieved.

The above is only possible when due attention is paid scientifically to other four concealed bodies in the gross physical body besides the physical body. In depth approach of the scientific development is needed at least in broad spectrum so that it must take care of all the bodies of the human system.

Disintegrated approach of medical care merely for the physical body healing may lead to the other complex disabilities of other hidden bodies that may lead to increase physical, mental and intellectual problems such that science will not be able to tackle easily this remedy in future.

So, firstly the close understanding of all the bodies of the human system must be perceived prior to deal with the integrated approach for the "whole" development.

The future research needs to be oriented in this integrated direction for happy growth of the human race. This will certainly lead to the extension of human life with proper health and well being.

Basically all the set norms for maintaining the physical well being must be followed; abdominal breathing pattern must be followed for better health; breath/prana should be diverted mentally to the unhealthy organ of the body.

A healthy physical and pure body transmits strength to the pranic body, which in turn gives the vitality to the mental body. This increases mental strength and makes the mind silent that increases its capacity and show right direction to mind by virtue of its cultivated silence.

Silence, in turn, assimilates pure knowledge in the mind that takes away all the vices of the mind gradually, and right positive illumination/knowledge pours in the mind.

Further more, meditation should be made un-deviated significant part of daily routine since meditation plays a major role in the direction of positive assimilation of thoughts; it gives very fine energy to the subtle systems of mind and intellect to make an accelerated progress to make them healthy, refined and strong.

All these consequently result in the dissolution of the egoistic nature of the self, and the soul/consciousness gradually starts having its positive influence on thoughts, words and deeds of an individual.

With time gradually soul is able to visualize its basic origin; this will enlighten the individual to choose the right and appropriate direction and he will cease to be the subordinate of his senses, and gradually he will lead happy and blissful life under the influence of manifested illuminated soul/consciousness without the effect of vices of the mind.

Meditation is the subtle food for subtle and causal bodies; it plays a vital role for the life extension, health, happiness and well being of physical human body. This acts like a catalyst to enhance the process of gradually conceiving life force, pranic energy and pure soul light.

Basically, it increases the consciousness level; manifested consciousness is transformed in super-consciousness; and finally soul/consciousness is transformed in divine light before it becomes part of "Being", the Supernal.

In this state time is transcended; and then with discontinuities whole process gets repeated. Thus with time, in time-less frame consciousness/self gets more refined vibrations; it gets manifested.

In this state divine energy is poured to human system automatically through apex centre. Gradually with time one will be able to feel this phenomenon. Appearance of life force manifested in meditation passes through various chakras; frequent movement of life force with discontinuity create divine energy in the chakras. This will make the body healthy and strong.

This finally acts as healing energy to all dormant subtle bodies of human system besides physical body. Apart from this, divine energy received from cosmos, being in stateless state of oneness with the "Being", manifest consciousness, and transmits pure power of divine healing to each cell since consciousness is spread every where in human body, all around us and in the entire universe.

Moreover in deep meditation as when one is beyond time; in timeless zone; when time is not felt; time is transcended; he is then beyond time & space; consciousness is then manifested it self; and divine healing energy is poured from cosmos that lead to extend the life of a human being with perfect health and happiness.

Under these conditions human breathe is calm and quite; it is in state of suspension. Without full co-operation of breathing process, there is no possibility of having control of mind and mergence of self in Self/supernal for manifestation of consciousness.

Furthermore, in the state of meditation, physical body is completely relaxed; mind is concentrated; it is one pointed; breathing process slows down; pulse rate of heart comes down. Even this achievement is the indication of life enhancement as per medical science.

Moreover in between the two breaths i.e. out going and the fresh breath that is on threshold to enter the human system, one remains without breathe for a fraction of a second. The interval without breath is the span of death.

In this discontinuity between the breaths i.e. in this interval one is in the state of unconsciousness; in this state of conscious-less; he is without breathe; he is beyond time & space; he is in the zone of Akaal; in timeless zone; he is in "Being", in the spirit/supernal unknowingly.

If consciously one can understand and experience this mystery of the divine nature, one can draw more energy consciously from cosmos. Unknowingly also, this energy is poured in the human system.

This divine energy gives grace to the concerned; heals each and every organ since it is spread all over in each cell of the body. Thus, the life is extended automatically by this energy along with manifestation of consciousness, which gets manifested in timeless zone.

Deep contemplation indicates that each one of us is in the blossom of death 21600 times per day i.e. the number of times one generally breaths; however this duration is extremely small. But, if it is integrated considering that one breathes approximately 10 times a minute, taking 6 seconds for each breath with a gap/interval of one second between the two consecutive breaths, then it is not difficult to assess that a person remains nearly 30 minutes without breath per day.

In other words, he is without breath, 15-20 hrs per month, about 8-10 days per annum; and in total life span of 80 years, about 800 days that is approximately 3% of the life span, he is without breath, with the death/spirit/Supernal in totality; he is in the zone of timeless; he is "Being", beyond time & space; he is unconscious and without breath. It is miraculous experience if one be conscious in this discontinuity.

By meditation and by consciously observing the breath one can extend this period even up to 10%-15% by reducing the number of breaths taken per minute; and subsequently the life span can be extended. In this interval, one is generally unconscious; he is conscious-less; he is in discontinuity; he is in on/off cycle of consciousness.

Thus he can be with the Supernal by his efforts and with the grace of "Being". During this period, he can instantaneously be beyond time & space.

Mind becomes very silent if consciously this discontinuity time interval is increased without any stress. It can even become the continuum experience to be with the Absolute; it is this discontinuity that makes a pathless path to be in unison with the "Being".

This helps to draw direct cosmic energy from the Absolute as and when it is needed by the system. Gradually system will be filled with divine light. This increases the life span; this makes him healthy, happy, peaceful and graceful. Thus, he can be with the source light of the Absolute; he can manifest his consciousness and enable to extend the healthy life to the maximum extent since positive energy is fed to all bodies of human system including gross, subtle and causal.

Thus, one can achieve extension of life through manifestation of consciousness; to be beyond time & space with discontinuities by taking step into "Being"; this will transform consciousness spontaneously in unconsciousness with discontinuity.

This will generate Sanjivini power i.e. life energy in the system. Rama used the same technique with his divine power to revive and rejuvenate Lakshmana when he was unconscious in war.

Also, as per Indian philosophy, one is born with fixed number of breaths. As the number of breaths consumed in life is exhausted, he has to leave the body; he dies. But by taking less number of breaths per minute, as explained above, it is natural that life span of an individual will increase.

Furthermore, taking breathe from right nostril, and mostly taking breathe from both nostrils; by keeping both nostril open and clean, divine energy enters the system. Thus tranquil breathing system is maintained that lead to increase the life span and continuously system is healed and is maintained healthy.

In the nutshell, the divine energy is drawn in discontinuities by mergence in "Being"; by mergence in breathing process; by discontinuity of flow of life force through various chakras through spinal cord etc. Also, by discontinuities in various processes of breathing exercises and by other multi-fold ways, the drawn divine energy is used to nourish all five human bodies to make them healthy.

Divine energy will manifest divine virtuous qualities in a human being through manifestation of consciousness; this will transmit healthier vibrations to each and every cell and give enormous pure healthier energy to the system; thus the healthier human life can be extended by divine energy.

This is the safest and reliable way of life extension by manifestation of consciousness; to be beyond time and space with discontinuities and to step in to "Being"; this transforms consciousness spontaneously in conscious-less with discontinuity. This gives supreme knowledge besides the life extension.

To summarize, one can easily visualize by the core analysis of this subject that health, happiness, well-being and transcendence are feasible through proper breathing and by having full command on breathing. Hence to say that "Breath is God" is not hyper projection of breathing.

36

Closure

The outstanding salient gists from the various chapters are expressed for refreshing; these are given to churn, understand and revolve around for deeper grasping; these are as follows:

1. Human consciousness and universal consciousness is basically the same; the difference is in degree of manifestation; universal consciousness is infinite where as human consciousness is finite.

2. Human soul is a source light; it is from Supernal; and it is the core consciousness in human being. Jeevatma is a personalized soul of human being with free will.

3. Mind is derivative of consciousness; it is the product of consciousness; mind gets energy from breathe; mind can be controlled by breathe; by suspension of breathe; mind is easily supervised by consciousness.

4. Mind is illusion/Maya. Illusion/Maya is a part of God. So, to control mind is possible by mercy of God.

5. Discontinuity is spontaneous void; it is instantaneous on & off; life after death is long discontinuity; it is wider void; energy is transmitted through discontinuity; it is Sandhya in Vedic language; it is the period of worship; there are four discontinuities in twenty four hours; in a year twelve discontinuities exist.

6. Human system gets divine energy from discontinuity between breathes in and breathe out; being with this discontinuity one

can be healthy, happy and can extend his life; for well being and self-realization, this is an asset.

7. Beyond time and space, in timeless zone, self being is with universal "Being"; one is conscious-less spontaneously; separateness is dissolved; one becomes "whole"; in this discontinuity divine energy is drawn and self consciousness is manifested. This is the secret of health, happiness and well being. Without having proper command on breathing, this state cannot be achieved.

8. Annihilation of mind renders silence; silence leads to manifest the consciousness by being conscious-less and by dissolving separateness and becoming "whole" in discontinuities. Mind has close link with breathing process.

9. Udana Prana/life force is to be generated in human system by close interaction of different Pranas in the system. Propagation of life force magnetizes the system and cures the ailments. It strengthens physical, pranic, mental, intellectual and spirit bodies of the system. Life force is the derivative of breath. Basically, breath is a part of cosmic energy.

10. Enlightenment gives booming divine energy to system, which is the source of health, happiness, well-being and cause of extension of human life besides knowledge and wisdom. Breath control plays a major role in this achievement.

11. Control on stresses can be achieved by generation of life force in the system; and revolving it frequently through the spinal cord. Abdominal breathing is the source to control stresses. Abdominal breathing helps the appearance of life force/ Udana Prana.

12. Fate can be modulated and effect of unknown forces can be minimized through stepping in beyond time & space. Step into "Being" is assisted by breathe control.

13. Life is continuum with discontinuities; every action will have reaction but it is governed by Newton's laws but with inertia effect of time delay.

14. Divine romance is the mysterious romance, which gives pure subtle energy for healing, well being and life extension. It assists in manifestation of human consciousness and being beyond time & space. It is the thread of self-realization. Life force and suspension of breath is the cause of divine romance.

15. Sub conscious mind acts as data bank for the conscious mind. Both exist very closely.

16. Flow of breath from left nostril indicates existence of mental energy in the system where as flow of breath from right nostril is indicative of spiritual energy. However, when there is free flow of breath in both nostrils, it is termed as tranquil breath; one is in harmonious state and can effortlessly meditate in this state; this state gives health, happiness, well being and longevity of life besides deep awareness.

17. Brahma manifested the Maya/illusion. It is the part of Brahma/God. Un-manifested God has created Maya as the separate manifested duality for His own play. It is mutative identity; it is itself a separate awareness. Maya/illusion is individual consciousness; it is part of Brahma. Through non-local process being with cosmic consciousness transcending time and space, it can be transformed to conscious-less.

18. Dispassion is gift of "Being". It assists to take step in to "Being" and lead to manifest consciousness.

19. There are four dormant bodies under the sheath of physical human body: Pranic; Mental; Intellectual and Spirit. Health and happiness of human being depends on the well-being of all the five bodies of human system. In subtle way breath connects all the bodies.

20. There are five Pranas in the human system: Prana; Apana: Vyana: Samana and Udana. They are transformed from breathe in human system through mysterious divine process.

21. Manifestation of consciousness by taking step into "Being" and transcendence of time & space act as catalyst to dissolve accumulated vices and tendencies as well help to control the

anger; blaming others; and in turn it will develop liking by all, prosperity, love, happiness, health, well-being in life, longevity and wisdom. Breath is a ladder to achieve subtle qualities.

22. Pranayama gives health and happiness besides it takes us beyond time & space; manifest consciousness and extend life; it is the controlled breathing process.

23. To take step into "Being" and to be beyond time & space will render deep Enlightenment of Mystery of death; death in life; death within; life in death; and Experience of life in death. Breath acts as a bridge between these states.

24. The soul coupled with awareness/consciousness or entangled with Maya/illusion Turns to be Jeevatma i.e. personalized soul; on the contrary, when Jeevatma loses Awareness/consciousness, it becomes pure soul. However, there is no life without Consciousness.

25. Astral travel is illusion/Maya; it does not help to manifest consciousness; it has no contribution in manifestation of consciousness, well-being and life extension.

26. Lack of spiritual energy in the human being increases the cosmic unbalance of pure positive energies, and if this spiritual energy increases by the positive efforts of the mankind, this will resolve number of problems and issues of the present generation.

27. Kundalini power is dormant in human being. This power is needed for spiritual evolution. Life force helps to awaken the unconscious Kundalini power. Without life forces one cannot transcend time & space and manifest his consciousness.

28. Relaxation is very significant but it cannot take beyond time & space; it cannot evolve, in hence creativity, manifest consciousness and it cannot be a tool for life extension. Relaxation is achieved by proper breathing process; it enhances general happiness, health and well being.

29. One must not be scared of various illusive problems and pitfalls in the journey beyond "time & space". These are insignificant before the highest achievement in the forefront of life.

30. Before transcendence of consciousness to "time & space", generally strong feeling at the apex centre is experienced; after this breathe is completely annihilated or it flows with discontinuity; then only transcendence of consciousness in cosmic consciousness with discontinuity is felt like on/off. But, no one can communicate when it is completely one with infinite consciousness since in that period he is conscious-less.

31. All sensations are perceived by mind and determined/analyzed by Buddhi/intellect and executed by Ahamkara/ego. By consciousness, being light source, all are illuminated. However, mind cannot perceive any thing beyond time, Space and causation.

32. Love, emotion and devotion are beyond self creation; their appearance is natural when there is immense heart to heart contact. Under the deep influence of these subtle qualities, one can effortlessly transcend time & space to manifest consciousness. The same happens when one is engrossed in present; his concentration/awareness increases; illusion/Maya disappears; mind is annihilated; breathe is suspended; he then steps in time-less zone to manifest consciousness.

33. The quantum jumping may be called the "human thought transference" process to enhance subtle qualities. It is means to manifest consciousness to jump beyond time & space to be with the "Being".

34. Synchronous breath pattern gives an edge to get involved smoothly with people of different temperaments as and when required; it transforms the personality spontaneously to manage the situation. One needs to have manifested awareness to deal with the synchronous breath pattern.

35. One can dissolve his built in egoism by transcending time and space; by step in "Being" and by cultivating subtle qualities in life through art of breathing and meditation.

36. Boredom in life can be transcended by engaging himself in activity of liking and by trapping subtle energy by witnessing the flow of breath in and out.

37. The safest and reliable way of life extension, heath, happiness and well-being is by controlled breathing and manifestation of consciousness; to be beyond time and space with discontinuities and to step in to "Being"; this transforms consciousness spontaneously to conscious-less state with discontinuity, and manifests consciousness in awaking state.

38. Manifested consciousness gives supreme knowledge besides the life extension, health, happiness and well - being. Breath plays a major role; breath is life and it is not out of the way to say that breath is God. Breath is secret of life.

Glossary

Advaita: (Literally non-dual). A School of Vedanta holding the oneness Of God, Soul and Universe.

Ahamkara: Ego.

Ajna/Agna: A psychic centre in the middle of the eyebrows; the seat of extra- sensory perception, higher intuitive perception and intelligence.

Akaal: The timeless being; God; omnipresent; infinity; existence.

Akasha: The first of the five material elements that constitute the universe, often translated as "space" and "Ether". The four other elements are Vayu (Air), Agni (Fire), Ap (Water) and Prithvi (Earth).

Anapanasati: Mindfulness of breathing; meditation on in- and-out breathing.

Anahata: A psychic centre situated at the heart level in the spinal column; the seat of creative power, unconditional love and compassion.

Apex centre: Highest centre: location of Sahasrara chakra.

Apara: Material knowledge.

Atman: The Self or Soul–denotes both the Supreme Self and the individual soul, which according to Advaita are identical as Brahman.

Atam-sakshatkara: God-realization

AUM:	The same as "OM".
Avidya:	A term of Vedanta denoting ignorance.
"Being":	Almighty; God.
Bhagavad Geeta:	An important Hindu Scripture containing the teaching of Lord Krishna to Arjuna.
Bhagti:	The yoga of love and devotion.
Brahma:	Name given to God signifying His aspect as Creator (one of the Hindu Trinity).
Brahman:	The Absolute or Supreme Reality.
Buddhi:	Determinative faculty of the mind; intellect.
Causal:	It is referred to the highest or inner most body that veils the atman or true soul.
Chaitanya:	Consciousness.
Chandra:	Moon.
Chakra:	Psycho-energy centre located in the spinal chord along the axis of a human body. There are seven chakras in human body.
Chhaya:	Shadow.
Chi:	Life force in Chinese culture as Prana in Indian culture; Qi—breath; energy; Ki in Japanese Culture; Qi in Korean culture.
Chida Akasha:	The sky of consciousness that is all permeating; the heart space in the head.
Chit:	The cognizing faculty.
Chit Vriti Nrodha:	Change of emotion as per will.
Chitta:	Mind with its accumulated impressions in its functions as memory.
Dhahra:	Anahata Chakra; heart chakra.
Dharma:	Righteousness.
Dharamayuddha:	Righteous war; fair war.

Dhyana:	The scientific art of mastering the mind; meditation; continuous awareness on a given subject.
Dwaita:	(Literally dual). A system of Philosophy holding that the Individual Souls are different from each other and from God.
Eshwara:	The Lord of the entire universe.
Guna:	Quality; it is of three types i.e. Satva, Rajas and Tamas. Tamas means dullness or inertia. Rajas mean restlessness or activity. Satva Means righteousness. Three qualities bind the human nature to the world.
Guna-tita:	Transcending all the qualities of Satva, Rajas and Tamas.
Guru:	Spiritual teacher or Preceptor; the remover/dispeller of darkness or ignorance; guide.
Ichha:	Desired.
Ida Nadi:	A nerve, which starts at the Mooladhara and runs to the left of Sushummna Nadi and ends at the right nostril.
Jagrit:	The waking state of consciousness.
Japa Yoga:	Chanting of Mantras or names of God; union with God through the process of repeating the names of God mentally or with rosary.
Jiva:	(Literally the living being). The individual soul; the embodied of living being.
Jeevan Mukta:	Liberated soul.
Jitendrya:	Winner of dynamic desires.
Jivatman:	The individual soul, which in essence is one with universal soul.
Jnana/Gnana:	Knowledge of Reality arrived at through reasoning and discrimination.

Jnanendriya/ Gnanendriyas:	Sabda(Sound), Sparsha(Touch), Roopa (Sight), Rasa (Taste) and Gandha (Smell).
Karana Sharira:	The Causal body.
Karma:	Action in general; duty.
Karma Yoga:	The path of selfless service.
Kriya:	Practical yoga technique; activity with awareness.
Kriya Yoga:	The scientific art of perfect God-Truth Union developed by Babaji.
Kula Chakra:	Chakras below Manipura namely Muladhara and Swadhisthanam.
Kumbhak:	Retention of breath.
Kundalini:	The name given to the energy being coiled and dormant at the base of the spinal system/ column.
Lambika Chakra:	Located between Visuddhi and Ajna chakras.
Laya:	Mergence.
Maha:	Big; great.
Manipura:	A psychic centre at the navel inside the spinal column; the seat of dynamic will, energy and action.
Mantra:	Seed words or sacred words constantly repeated by the mind; this may open the consciousness to a higher level and which frees one from the bondage of habitual tendencies.
Mauna:	Silence.
Maya:	A term of Vedantic philosophy denoting ignorance, obscuring the vision of reality. The cosmic illusion on account of which one appears as many. It is illusion; it has multiple meaning depending on the text.

Muladhara:	Root chakra; one of the seven chakras.
Nadi:	Energy channel in the human body.
Nirvana:	Final absorption in Brahman, or all pervading reality through the annihilation of the individual ego.
Nirvikalpa/ Samadhi:	State of absolute nothingness.
Om:	(also known as Pranava). It is most sacred word of the Vedas; it is also As AUM. It is symbol both of the personal God and the Absolute.
Para:	Beyond; spiritual knowledge; the causal aspect of Sound.
Para Mauna:	Absolute silence.
Paramatman:	The Universal or Supreme Soul.
Pawanjaya:	Command of breath.
Pingala Nadi:	A nerve, which runs at right side of the Sushumna Nadi and ends at the left nostril.
Prana:	It is Life Force energy that sustains breath in a physical body. Prana further subdivided in Apana, Vyana, Samana and Udana for executing various functions of the body.
Pranayama:	The scientific art of mastering/regulation of the breath.
Prarabdha:	Karmas, which are part of the sanchit karmas i.e. a collection of past karmas (good or bad deeds), ready to be experienced in the present body in this life.
Rishi:	A seer of truth to whom the wisdom of the Vedas was revealed.
Sadhak:	One who does Sadhana/austerities.

Sadhana: Discipline; all that one does to remember Truth, the Self or God.

Sage: One who experiences God-realization in the intellectual plane.

Sahasrara: "One thousand"; the chakra or psycho-energy center, which encompasses the brain and extends above the head; the center of cosmic consciousness.

Saint: One who experiences God-realization in the spiritual plane of existence.

Sakshi Chaitanya: Conscious awareness.

Sam Yami Lakshana: Symptoms of controlling thoughts.

Samadhi: A super-conscious state; an objective of meditation; transcending of three known states of consciousness i.e. waking, dreaming and dream-less sleep; breathless state of communion with God; yogic trance; calm; desire-less self- awareness; mergence and self poise; self-realization.

Samatha/

Samsara: It is the Buddhist practice of calming of the mind by practicing single-The material world; unceasing cycle of births and deaths.

Samyami Sadhana: Discipline for increased life span.

Sandhya: Worship at the time of sunrise, noon and sunset; it is transition time.

Sangarama: War.

Sanjivani: A cure–plant which can reverse even death.

Sankalpa: Determination to perform.

Sat-Chit-Ananda: It is Existence-Consciousness-Bliss. It is name of Brahman or Absolute Reality.

Satsang: Fellowship with truth seeker.

Satvik: See Guna; it is philosophy to achieve truth, consciousness and Bliss.

Savikalpa Samadhi: Absoption in Brahman where consciousness of duality and multiplicity remains.

Shakti: Energy; the great universal power; the Divine mother.

Shamatha: Pointed meditation through mindfulness of breathing.

Sharnagati: Surrender in devotion.

Shavasa: Breath.

Shiva: Name of the God of dissolution.

Shunayaka: Emptiness; voidness; spaciousness; a state of vacuum without air in the system.

Shushumna Nadi: A central nerve running through the spinal column, starting from Mooladhara and flanked by the Ida and Pingala Nadis to its left and right sides.

Shushupti: The third states of consciousness of deep and dreamless sleep; yogic rest.

Sloka: Verse of two lines in praise of God.

Subtle: Psycho-spiritual constituent of living beings according to esoteric, occult and mystic teaching.

Supernal: Almighty; God.

Surya: Sun.

Swadhistanam: A psychic centre between Mooladhara and Manipur centres; it is at the base of the sexual organ; near the coccyx.

Swapna: The dreaming state of consciousness.

Trinity: Mergence with God, the Supernal; God the father, the son and the Holy Spirit are each equally and eternally the one true God.

Turiya: It is the state of Samadhi; it is the fourth state of cosciousness; it is transcendence of waking, dreaming and dream-less sleep.

Udana Prana: One of the five division of Prana; it moves upward.

Unmani Chakra: When consciousness in meditation reaches to thousand petal led Lotus, it is crosses the to eighth lotus; this is called Unmani Chakra; it is position of no mind.

Vipassana: Inside awareness.

Vishuddhi: The chakra or psycho-energy in the cervical plexus, opposite the throat; seat of visualization; psychic communication.

Yoga: The scientific art of perfect God-Truth union; the union of individual soul with the infinite, eternal being, consciousness and bliss.

Books Published by Author

Technical Books by Author